DEDICATION

This book is dedicated to the dedicated men and the dedicated women who, as dedicated computer programming professionals, dedicate themselves to working in Information Technology groups that are dedicated to providing dedicated services to dedicated organizations who fully dedicate their resources to their dedicated missions.

It Only Hurts When I Hit <ENTER>

Michael A. Raithel

CONTENTS

ACKNOWLEDGMENTS

My first thank you goes to freelance editor Paul Betz for the great job he did editing my use of the English language.

I owe Lorena Friess a debt of gratitude for her tireless work on getting the front cover picture(s(s(s(s)))) just right.

Thanks go to long-time colleague and friend Mike Rhoads for providing valuable feedback on a rough draft of my manuscript.

Big appreciations go to Hipgnosis (Storm Thorgerson and Audrey Powell) for introducing me to the Droste effect via the front cover of Pink Floyd's 1969 **Ummagumma** album. I have enjoyed looking at that cover for dozens of years.

A shout out goes to the writers at owlcation.com for the well-written article on determining the number of candies in a container (https://owlcation.com/stem/How-to-Calculate-the-Number-of-MMs-in-a-Container). I wish that article had been available when the brainiacs at the data center were trying to work out their practical math problem.

Finally, I would like to thank all of the sinners and the saints; the nerds and the straight arrows; the techies and the know-nothings; the slackers and the authoritarians; the brilliant and the intellectually challenged; the programmers and the users that I have worked with in offices, cubicle farms, and data centers for entertaining me in *both* senses of the word.

I INTRODUCTION

Thanks to movies and television shows, many people believe that computer programmers are quirky, geeky, asocial nerds who have the power to retrieve every conceivable type of information. Some think that we can surface the pictures, personal histories, and financial records of any person in the world. Many believe we can call up the architectural plan of all existing buildings in order to examine the detailed layout of every floor, discover long-forgotten underground passageways, and determine which air vents are large enough for a person to crawl through. Others think we can dig up anybody's criminal history, including mugshots, an itemized list of infractions, and every criminal association they ever had. And some believe that we can hack into every existing computer system and that we are all well practiced in yelling out: *I'm in!*

When computer programmers try to describe what it is that they actually do at work, we often get puzzled looks and general incomprehension. Sometimes we also get light-hearted ridicule and teasing. For example, a married man arriving home from an exhilarating day of programming might tell his wife:

"What a day! I wrote a program that opened a directory of newly cleaned data sets, accessed two large files, and bulk-loaded the contents into a database. Then I accessed the database and created a new table!"

And his wife might respond with something like this:

"That's nice dear. While you are waiting for dinner, open the dishwasher of newly cleaned dishes, access the two large racks and bulk-load the contents into a kitchen cabinet. Then access the cupboards and set the dining room table."

Relatedly, a full stack developer dining out with her boyfriend might carefully consider her answer when he asks how her workday went. She probably wouldn't exclaim:

"Work was great! I finally completed the User Interface, did some significant work on the API, performed some Linux shell scripting, and applied two patches to the Apache web server."

He just wouldn't understand. More than likely she would say something like this:

"Not bad; I had good day. Hey, would you like some of my salad?"

An applications programmer watching a football game with a group of his friends would have a similar problem sharing a work-related joke. For example, things might go something like this:

After the first quarter, his attorney friend tells the joke about a lawyer, a doctor, and an accountant in a lifeboat in shark-infested waters. Everybody laughs. After the second quarter, his insurance salesman friend tells the joke about the traveling salesman and the farmer with seven daughters. Everybody laughs. After the third quarter, his family therapist friend tells the joke about the geriatric couple who walk into a psychiatrist's office. Everybody laughs. After the fourth quarter; the programmer just can't resist. He has read the funniest joke on a techie listserv and knows that they are going to like it. So he says: *"Guys, guys, I've got one: A SQL query walks into a bar. It approaches two tables and asks: Do you mind if I join you?"*

Nobody laughs. They all look at him with puzzled expressions for a moment. Then they shake their heads and head into the kitchen for more pizza, wings, and beer. They just don't get it.

But we get it, don't we? Computer programmers know why *that* joke is funny. Computer programmers know why the joke about the PC CD-drive being used as a cup holder is funny. Computer programmers know why the joke about the "extroverted" programmer being the one who looks at *your shoes when he is talking to you* is funny. Computer programmers know why the joke about *how many programmers it takes to change a lightbulb* is funny. But well-worn jokes aside, we know that the best computer-related humor comes from the idiosyncratic behavior of our colleagues, management, clients, and institutions. That is truly where the best jokes lie.

The 2^4 stories in this book really occurred. I masked, scrambled, swapped, and perturbed the names of people and organizations in order to protect the innocent, the guilty, and the hapless bystanders who were neither. Because I enjoy my current job, I assiduously avoided including any stories related to my employer in any way, shape, or form in this book. Nonetheless, you could easily . . .

What's that?

Oh, okay!

I had planned to write a longer Introduction, but the leader of the black ops team that has been patiently waiting for me to finish writing this just told me that I need to hack into the secret installation's computer system, kill the current in the electric fence, compromise the motion detectors, and bring the security cameras down so that they can facilitate a stealthy entry via the long-forgotten sewer passages I found online.

Accessing the gateway now . . .

Only a few more mouse clicks . . .

Wait for it . . .

Almost there . . .

I'm in!

You don't believe a word of that last bit do you? Ah, then you must be a computer programmer!

0000 THE INTERVIEW FROM HELL

I probably never would have put up with their crap if I had not needed the job so badly. I was a college senior majoring in computer science looking for my first computer programming job. All of the want ads for junior programmers stated that at least one year's worth of programming experience was required from prospective job candidates. But this small firm in a nearby town had advertised for an entry-level programmer with the only requirement being a degree in computer science. Bingo!

On the day of my interview, I arrived early at the firm's offices with my professors' recommendations and my college transcript in hand. I was wearing the best clothes that I owned at the time — a Sunday suit, white shirt, blue tie, and black shoes — and my hair was newly cut and neatly combed. The receptionist had me fill out a personal information form and job application. Once that was done, I waited. And waited. And waited some more. About an hour after my stated appointment time, Biff came to the reception area, introduced himself, and led me to the interview room.

The interview room was a large conference room with the lights dimmed almost to twilight. I was directed to sit on one side of the conference table. On the other side sat Biff, Bill, and Murphy. Biff and Bill were in their mid-to-late twenties, while Murphy was middle aged. Biff and Bill were programmers; Murphy was the manager of the programming staff.

"We like to do group interviews," Biff explained. "That way, we can see how a candidate reacts under pressure."

"But first, arrange these cards in your order of color preference," said Bill handing me a deck of ten cards. The cards were white with a big colored square in the center of one side. Each card had a different color on it: red, blue, green, purple, and so on.

"That is, put down the card with the color you like the most first, then the one you like the next-to-most, etc. The card with the color that you like the least should be on the top."

I arranged the cards in the order that appealed to me and handed them to Bill. He retreated to the end of the table and started comparing them to some kind of booklet that he had there, taking notes on a legal pad.

"Hmm . . . interesting," he muttered.

"Okay, let's get started," Bill said when he finally returned from the end of the table. Then, he looked me directly in the eyes and asked me a moderately difficult computer programming question.

I had barely answered the question when Biff cut me off with another quick-fire question. My answer to the second question had hardly left my mouth when Murphy shot out a complicated programming question. And that is how it went for half an hour: rapid-fire question after rapid-fire question; sometimes obvious; sometimes complicated; sometimes open-ended; sometimes very specific; sometimes argumentative; sometimes condescending; with my answer to a previous question many times cut off. And, all the while, the three of them were staring so intently across the table at me that I almost felt like they were trying to hypnotize me.

"Okay, so much for your programming knowledge, let's see how logically you think," Biff finally said, signaling the end of the technical interview.

"Imagine a pure white marble cube floating in the air above this table. Imagine drawing tic-tac-toe lines on one side of the cube and also on the top of the cube. Then imagine cutting along those lines completely through the cube, first cutting through the side and then cutting through the top. Once you have done that along the four lines on the side and the four lines on the top, you levitate the resulting cubes away from the original mass. How many individual white cubes will you now have?"

Desperate for the job, I had been concentrating so hard on every word that Biff said that I could totally visualize the dissected white cube floating above the desk.

"There would be twenty-seven individual white cubes," I said.

"Okay. Okay, fine." Biff continued. "Imagine that those cubes are now put back together so that they form the big cube again. Now, the big cube is slowly lowered into a bucket of red paint. It is levitated back up into the air and allowed to dry. Next, the pieces are taken back apart. Got it?"

"Yes, I think that I understand," I said, having no idea where this was going.

"Okay. Good. Now, how many of the cubes will be red on three sides?" Bill asked.

"Um . . . eight," I replied doing the picture-calculation in my head.

"How many would be red on one side?" belted out Biff.

"There would be . . . ah . . . that would be six," I replied through my deep concentration on the image.

"How many cubes would not have a red side at all?" Murphy rapid-fired in my direction.

"Only one," I promptly replied. I had been waiting for that question.

"Okay. Okay fine," Biff said smirking. "How many cubes would be red on only *two* sides?"

"Um, let's see . . . ," I said, trying to get it straight in my head. At that point, I was panicking. It was hard for me to keep that entire image in my mind and count the red sides. I went over it again and again under their uncompromising, pitiless, smug stares.

"He's stalling," said Bill.

"Um, that would be about . . ."

"He doesn't know," laughed Murphy.

"C'mon, c'mon, we don't have all morning," Biff urged, leaning forward across the table.

Finally, I thought that I had it.

"Okay, that would be . . . um, eight," I said.

"Bzzt!" exclaimed Biff. "Try again."

"Would it be nine?" I asked with the desperation rising.

"Bzzt! Try again," Biff taunted.

"He's just guessing now," said Murphy in a disgusted and dismissive tone.

"C'mon now, think. Think. Think!" urged Biff, raising his voice louder with each "think."

"Yeah, think! Think hard!" said Bill, leaning forward over the table as if trying to force the answer out of me.

I fought through my panic and did think. I thought hard. I thought very, very hard.

"Oh, right. There would be twelve cubes with red on two sides," I finally blurted out.

"Right!" the three of them exclaimed, practically in unison. They all sat back, and the tension seemed to evaporate from the room.

I felt elated that I had figured it out and dropped back into my chair, exhausted.

"There is one final thing that you need to do before we conclude the interview," Bill said. He shuffled the ten color-coded cards and handed them back to me.

"Arrange these cards in your order of least preference. That is, put down the card with the color you *do not* like the most first, then the one you don't like the next-to-most, etc. The card with the color that you like the best should be on the top."

I put the cards face up on the table and tried to arrange them in the reverse order that I had originally put them into at the beginning of the interview. But I was not sure whether I was successful or not. Finally, I handed the cards back to Bill.

"Hmmm . . . ," he said rifling through them, "interesting."

Everybody stood up, signaling that the interview was over. They each reached across the table and shook hands with me.

"Thanks for coming in," said Murphy. "We are interviewing other candidates and expect to have our final decision next Friday."

I left the interview with my head swimming. I couldn't tell whether I had been successful or not. I was so stressed out and mentally exhausted that I skipped my late-afternoon computer science class and just went home to chill out.

I did not hear back from them the next Friday. So, I called the following Monday to inquire about my candidacy. But neither Biff, nor Bill, nor Murphy was available to take my call. I left a message. I sweated out the week waiting for a return call that never came. The next week, I called several times and left several messages that went unanswered. Towards the end of that week, I finally caught Bill on the phone. He told me that they were still trying to decide among a host of good candidates and that I was definitely one of them. Another week passed with me agonizing over whether or not to call. I finally did and got Biff on the line.

"Oh, didn't anybody tell you?" he asked. "We gave that job to somebody else two weeks ago. Sorry that nobody got back to you. Hey, good luck with your job search."

***

Several years later, I was a rising, hotshot junior programmer with lots of experience and a deep love for *all-things-programming*. I saw an interesting advertisement from a firm that was looking for a team leader to supervise a group of application programmers on a new project. The project was state-of-the-art, the company was known as a good employer for the area, and the advertised pay range would have provided a definite step up from my current salary. So, I applied for the position, heard back from them, and went in for an interview.

I filled out the usual background information form and job application form in the personnel department reception area. Then I was ushered into the office of the manager who was going to interview me. We shook hands, and I sat down in the chair in front of his desk, getting myself ready for the interview.

"Let me tell you how we are going to do this," he said, leaning back in his chair. "I am going to ask you a few questions about your background and then about your salary expectations. Then we will go to the conference room for a group interview."

"Group interview?" I asked.

"A couple of the managers and I like to collectively interview our job candidates," he said. "Not only do we want to make sure that they know their stuff, but we want to see how they react under pressure."

"Hey, wait! Where are you going?" he asked as I slid out of the chair, turned on my heels, and went out the door.

I never looked back.

0001 MUCH ADO ABOUT NOTHING

It was my first computer programming job, and I was happy to have it. I had just graduated with a degree in computer science into a job market where every programming job advertisement demanded a year's worth of previous programming experience. But how do you get a year's worth of programming experience when nobody will give you the opportunity to program without your already having a year's worth of programming experience? Conundrum, right? Right! Fortunately, a small, minority-owned consulting firm gave me a break and hired me as a junior programmer. I was assigned to work on their big contract at a federal agency located in downtown Washington, DC.

The office was situated below street level in the bowels of a massive federal building. Most days, we entered the office area by walking down the ramp to the loading dock, going through the large loading doors, threading our way between the pallets of supplies, and then cutting through the stairwell to the office space. The badly recycled air often smelled of diesel fuel, the lighting in the offices and corridors was dim, the furniture was well-worn and outdated, the carpeting was rutted and balding, and stacks of old computer printouts and reports were piled high in every office and corridor. Many of the government workers and some of the other consultants grumbled about the work environment. But I didn't mind; it was my first computer programming job and I was happy.

My assignment was to take over the maintenance of a dozen computer programs that reported on the funding of grants given to local public works projects all over the country. They were government grants for things like building playgrounds, creating new parks, cleaning up public spaces, and so on. The monthly reports provided details about the money allocated, money spent, and money left over for the hundreds and hundreds of public works projects. The reports were shipped to the local congressmen and congresswomen so that they could keep track of what monies were going to their individual districts.

The computer programs were written in the Common Business-Oriented Language (COBOL), a popular programming language of the time. They were hundreds of lines long and very complicated. My half-dozen predecessor programmers had added to and patched the code so many times that it had become what we referred to as *spaghetti code*. The programming flow was very twisted and intertwined, making the logic very hard to follow. In addition to that, the previous programmers had not been diligent about adding comments to the programs. So, the only way to really follow the logic was to sight-read the programming code and mentally keep track of what was going on. And, as an added challenge, my predecessors had not used meaningful variable names. So, it was hard to keep track of the hundred or so main variables that were assigned and reassigned values throughout the many, many lines of programming code. But I didn't mind; it was my first computer programming job and I was happy.

The programming was done on mainframe computers that were only accessible via a row of hard-wired computer terminals in a so-called Terminal Room. To access your programs on the mainframes, you had to reserve one of the 10 terminals in the Terminal Room. There was a sign-up sheet outside the Terminal Room door with a 12-hour grid for each of the 10 terminals. People would hurry in, first thing in the morning, and pick the time slots that they wanted. Sometimes, all of the slots for the 9-to-5 timeframe would be taken, and people would curse as they filled in the overtime slots. Occasionally, the terminal you signed up for would be down due to a hardware problem, and you had to stay later to use a different terminal. Sometimes, your programming tasks took longer than you expected, and you had to stay later to catch a free terminal. But I didn't mind; it was my first computer programming job and I was happy.

I pretty much lived inside the dozen COBOL programs that were under my control. I printed them out on green-bar paper, annotated the printouts with scores of notes, and then read and reread them. I added comments to the sections of the programs that I understood. I created flowcharts of the program flow to map out what was really going on in the programs. I renamed variables so that they had names that reflected the piece of information they were holding. I untangled the spaghetti code whenever I got a chance, so that the programs flowed more logically. I brought the printouts home with me to study at night and on the weekends. That irked my girlfriend and confused my friends, who all thought that I was spending way too much time thinking about work. But I didn't mind; it was my first computer programming job and I was happy.

After I had been on the job for about three months, Mr. Bradford transferred to another government agency. Mr. Bradford was the administrator in charge of the public works programming tasks. He attended all of the public works administration meetings and translated changing federal requirements into specifications. He provided written specs on what needed to be changed in the computer programs to keep them in line with current laws. Mr. Bradford also supplied the input on which new districts or congressmen/women needed to be added and which ones needed to be removed from the reports. On the first Tuesday of every month, when the twenty-or-so boxes of reports rolled off of the printers, they were delivered to Mr. Bradford's office. He spent a couple of days directing his subordinates in the effort of separating the reports from various districts and getting them shipped out to those districts. Sometimes, when he was short-staffed, he asked me to pitch in even though I had programming work to do. But I didn't mind; it was my first computer programming job and I was happy.

About four months after he had left, I happened to walk into Mr. Bradford's old office to look for an old spec. They had not found a replacement for him, and the office had been dark since he had left. I was shocked at what I saw when I switched the light on. Covering almost half of the floor space in the office were scores and scores of boxes containing the public works reports. I looked at the labels on the boxes and saw that they held the reports for every month since Mr. Bradford had left. None of them had been sent out. I went next door to the office of the person who had reported to Mr. Bradford and told her about the reports. She said that she was aware of the problem, but that Mr. Bradford had not provided written directions on what was to be done with them. Furthermore, she told me, nobody contacted the office to ask why they had not received a report in over four months. Nobody had called, nobody had written, nobody had stopped by. Nobody!

I went back to my office stunned. I thought about all of the work I had been doing untangling the spaghetti code. I thought about all of the work I had done flowcharting the program flow and untangling the logic. I thought of all of the work I had done annotating printouts of the programs. I thought about all of the work I had done renaming variables. I thought about all of the times that I had taken the programs home to study at night and on weekends. And I thought about all of the times that I had helped separate and collate the reports while my programming assignments were pending. I *did* mind; it was my first computer programming job and I was *unhappy*.

Two months later, I was working somewhere else.

0010 THE MEETING ROOM

To appreciate this story — *to really appreciate it* — you need to clearly see with your mind's eye the meeting room itself. Picture a large three-story ballroom in a federal government building in the heart of Washington, DC. Along one wall there were floor-to-ceiling windows. Along the opposing wall there was a 16-by-8-foot white marble balcony jutting out from the second floor. The balcony was accessible from curved marble staircases on each side. The organization had needed office space to staff the administration of a new two-year social program. Being tight on office space, they turned the ballroom into a vast maze of cubicles and cleverly installed a small men's room and matching women's room in the space beneath the balcony. They completed the redesign by putting a long meeting table and a group of chairs on the balcony, turning it into an open-air meeting room.

On a typical Washington, DC, hazy, hot, and humid July afternoon, we were called to a meeting in the balcony meeting room to discuss changes to one of the social program's computer applications. Two of my fellow programmers and I climbed the stairs and made ourselves comfortable at the table. Also present were a few social program staff members whom we knew, as well as a few we did not know. We exchanged pleasantries, got our pens and writing pads ready, and waited for the meeting to begin. Not yet on hand was the Assistant Director, who was to lead the meeting.

As we sat in silence, we heard the door to a stall in the men's room directly below us close. Prior to that meeting, I had not noticed that noises from the restrooms were quite that clear on the balcony. We heard the toilet seat drop down rather hard. The initial conversations had died out. Some people were looking at their notes, and others were doodling in their notepads. Then we heard the first salvo of noises from the bathroom. The acoustics were astounding!

There was a loud grunt. Then there was a prolonged and drawn out "unh." People in the meeting room looked blankly past one another or down at their notepads, trying with great deliberation to show that they were not listening. We were, after all, a group of polite Washington, DC, federal workers and contractors. But the performance only got louder and more profound.

There came a series of loud, expository explosions. There were toots; there were whistles; there were pops; there were sputters; there were high octaves and low, wavering bass notes. There were grunts and groans and long, guttural exhalations. A cadence of sharp pachyderm sounds gave way to an extended aria of high-pitched whines that sounded like a jet engine warming up. Amid the chaotic sounds, the bellow of an angry moose switched abruptly to the sound of a goose in its death throes.

I looked up from my notepad to see that several people were shaking violently with silent, unsuccessfully held-back laughter. Then one of the women in the group broke out with a loud guffaw. Suddenly, the entire group—myself included—was laughing hysterically at the crystal-clear orchestrations that were coming from below. We laughed until tears ran down our eyes, and we almost fell out of our chairs. We laughed until the rolling of a toilet paper dispenser and the flushing of a toilet finally ended the unholy symphony coming from beneath us.

The laughter died out, and we regained our composure, exchanging smirking, knowing looks with one another. Then somebody came bounding up the marble staircase. It was the Assistant Director. He took his place at the head of the table.

"Sorry I'm late," he said. "I had to stop by the men's room on my way here."

He stared blankly and uncomprehendingly as the table erupted into a mass of hysterical, sidesplitting laughter.

0011 A DAY LATE AND A DOLLAR SHORT

He was a belligerent, bellicose, bombastic, train-wreck of a man with a ruddy round face, bleary gray eyes, thinning oily black hair, and a once-broken boozy nose. He towered over us at six-foot-something in his trademark short-sleeved, sweat-stained white shirt, dime-store tie, and half-filled plastic pocket protector. He had large simian arms and held his hands cupped backwards at his sides as if constantly shielding a lit cigarette; he swung those arms in vigorous arcs as he walked. He thrust his face forward across his billowing midriff and practically into yours when he talked to you. I did not know whether he was born mean or whether his unfulfilled professional life had made him that way. Whatever the case, Derrick made our lives hell!

Derrick was the technical lead on an important IT project for a Fortune 100 company. He made it no secret that he thought he should be the project manager for the team of five employees and seven consultants. After all, he had many more years of computer programming experience than Tom, our long-suffering, politically correct, paper-pushing project manager. The project was "doomed to failure" because Tom was not listening to Derrick and not doing things Derrick's way. Instead, Tom was following corporate policy and using "new" computer technology—technology that was "not tried and true" and, coincidentally, that was not in Derrick's programming skill set. And worst of all, Tom had hired too many "damned consultants"! That is where I came in; I was a "damned consultant."

Actually, I was one of six damned consultants from a small, local consulting firm that had been hired to work on the six-to-eight-month-long project. We were a group of young computer programmers with coding experiences ranging from about three to seven years. The corporation that we were consulting at was a huge employer in the city, and our company considered this contract to be a very important gateway to future business. So, we could not afford to fail—for the sake of either our consulting company or our own nascent careers.

As I said, Derrick made our lives hell. He talked openly about what a waste of money it was for his organization to hire consultants when he could easily do the job of any two or three of us. He was always watching for mistakes in our flowcharts, our computer programs, out documentation, our code walk-throughs, our systems plans, and even gaps in our attendance. He would loudly announce a transgression to the whole listening world, concluding with his favorite rejoinder: "You're a day late and a dollar short, pal."

"Excuse me, Derrick, but when are the servers scheduled to be down for maintenance this week?"

"Do I look like I'm the damned Systems Engineer? Call Systems and find out yourself. You're a day late and a dollar short, pal!"

"Pardon me, Derrick, but what changes were just made to the systems plan? I need to make sure they are reflected in my program."

"I'll post the changes when I'm done making them and not a damn minute before! You're a day late and a dollar short, pal!"

"Um, Derrick, did you happen to finish creating the test data sets that we have been waiting for? Sorry, but we are really stuck on testing the suite of data editing programs until we get them."

"I've got too many damned things to do around here. I'll get to them when I get to them. I don't care what Tom told you; in my day we created our own test data sets, instead of sitting around twiddling our thumbs and waiting for *Mommy* to do it for us. You're a day late and a dollar short, pal!"

Despite his bellicose temperament, there was one person on the team whom Derrick never insulted, never mouthed off to, never ranted about, and never raged against: Jim. I think Derrick was a little bit afraid of Jim. That made sense because all of us were a little bit afraid of Jim. Jim was an independent contractor who had been brought onto the project as a senior programmer/analyst to write the code that interfaced with the database management system. There was nothing that you could tell Jim about the programming language, the operating system, the database management system, or the structured systems design methodology we were using that he didn't already know. He had been a successful independent computer consultant for many years. Perhaps he worked as a freelancer for the bigger paycheck, but I strongly suspected it was because Jim could not get along with anybody in a corporate environment.

Jim was about six-foot-four with unfashionably long blond hair, a blond beard, and cobalt blue eyes having that disturbing, penetrating, thousand-yard stare. He was a loner, a recluse, a quiet guy—as in that perennial quote you read in news stories: "*I don't know why he snapped; he was always such a quiet guy.*" When he did speak, it was slow, deliberate, and concise, as if he were choosing every word with infinite care. Jim never socialized with anybody in the office, preferring to be alone as much as possible. He sat programming in his cubicle all day long, rarely ventured out to the restroom, never went to the break area, and only grudgingly attended the Monday project status meeting. Jim openly flaunted the business-casual dress code by wearing what looked like the same pair of faded jeans, green polo shirt, and well-worn loafers every day. Because he would fix you with his intense, unblinking, withering gaze, we all avoided talking to him face-to-face, preferring to communicate via email as much as possible. One could easily imagine that at one time Jim had come to a fork in the road of his life where one path led to becoming a computer programmer and the other to becoming an ax murderer, and he had picked the computer programming route, but just barely.

Some things in life are inevitable. Water will always flow downhill from rivulets to creeks, to streams, to brooks, to rivers, and finally to the sea. That one small, pretty-much-cosmetic change you made to your computer program that shouldn't affect anything will end up causing a catastrophic, almost untraceable error the next time the program is run. The sun will rise in the east and set in the west. Once the programming has been completed on a tight-deadline project, the users will ask for "minor" must-have changes that destroy the entire logic structure and call for a total rewrite. The short line that you pick will always move slower than the longer ones around it because of difficult customers. The data set you received from a most trusted source will contain dirty data despite their assurances of stringent and rigorous QC. When you toss your cat over the sofa, he will always land on four feet. And so it was inevitable that a bombastic lout would be unable to help himself and strike out at a person who was not at all a safe target.

I got to work late one Monday morning due to a dental appointment and found the whole office buzzing with the news of what had just happened at the end of the project status meeting. Apparently, it had played out like this: *Tom asked Jim for his opinion on using a particular SQL technique for accessing the database. Jim answered in his slow, deliberate way, with the rest of the team leaning on his every word, as they always did. Derrick snorted his disapproval and provided an alternative approach. Uncharacteristically, Jim patiently explained why his method was more efficient. That's when Derrick crossed the line and told Jim that he didn't know what he was talking about and that he was "a day late and a dollar short, pal." Everybody gasped. Jim locked eyes with Derrick. He gave him a withering look that said, "One of these days, I'm going to cut you into little pieces." Derrick glared back with a look that said, "You could stand me up at the gates of hell, but I won't back down." They stared each other down in a contest of wills—one an inveterate bully; the other a potential serial killer. The room was deathly silent. A minute passed. The staring continued. Another excruciatingly silent minute passed, and the tension grew, and grew, and grew as everybody waited for the inevitable flashpoint. Finally, Derrick averted his gaze and looked down at his legal pad. A thin smile played across Jim's mouth. He capped his pen, closed his notebook, slid his chair back from the table, and slowly walked out of the meeting room.*

Word of the incident had spread faster than the norovirus, and the whole office was on edge for the rest of the day. I don't know exactly what we thought would happen, but we did think that *something* was going to happen—something loud, something ugly. But both of the combatants stayed out of sight in their respective cubicles. Derrick left at 5:00 pm as usual to catch his bus out of the city. I was absorbed in making a half-dozen user-requested changes to one of my big programs at about 7:00 pm when I heard the whirring click-click-click of Jim wheeling his 12-speed down the main hallway to the elevators. The next day passed without incident. So did the next. And the next day too. By Friday, everybody had forgotten about the confrontation, and the prevailing groupthink was to get out of the office early to begin enjoying what was shaping up to be an unseasonably great weather weekend.

The next week, Derrick's entire demeanor unexpectedly changed. He came in on Monday and whistled his way around the office. Our furtive glances in his direction verified that Derrick was actually cheerful and smiling. He was cordial and helpful in the morning project status meeting. On Tuesday, Derrick proactively updated the test data and sent us an email detailing how we could access it. On Wednesday, he sent us the system maintenance schedule and highlights of the changes to the system plan. On Thursday, Derrick took it upon himself to update a plethora of pending systems testing specs and sent us the links to them. But the thing that shocked us the most was when he came in that Friday dressed up in a suit. It was plaid and loud and just the thing you would picture Derrick wearing. But we had never seen him all dressed up before, and he affected a kind of tacky charm. Derrick left at lunchtime carrying a briefcase and did not return for the rest of the afternoon.

On Monday, Newton's Third Law — "For every action, there is an equal and opposite reaction" — came back to haunt us with a vengeance. Derrick arrived at work in a rage. He barged around the office, constantly muttered hateful things about consultants under his breath, threw his pen, banged his desk drawers shut, shouted at people over the telephone, and picked an argument with anybody unlucky enough to catch his eye in the hallways. He was totally out of control. Then, he finally went too far and derided Missy. None of us heard the first part of the confrontation, but we all heard Missy yell, "That's it. I am not going to take any more of your . . . your . . . stuff!" and several people saw her hurrying towards the elevators, apparently to lodge a complaint with the Human Resources Department on the fourth floor.

"Derrick! My office! Now!" we heard Tom command about a half hour later in a voice that said he was deadly serious.

"Yeah, damn straight!" Derrick yelled back at him.

I stood up and looked over the top of the cubicles to see what was happening. I saw that everybody else was standing up in their cubicles too, like an alerted prairie dog colony, facing Tom's glassed-walled office on the far side of the work area. We saw Tom, Derrick, and an unidentified woman in a smart blue business suit in Tom's office. The woman spoke for a minute. Derrick responded, gesturing wildly. Tom spoke for a minute. Derrick responded, gesturing wildly. The woman pointed at Derrick and said something loud. Derrick responded loudly. Tom pointed at Derrick and said something loud. Derrick responded so loudly that we could see both Tom and the woman recoil. Derrick suddenly turned and burst out of Tom's office, slamming the door against the outer wall. The last part of his final, over-the-shoulder rejoinder resounded throughout the office: ". . . and you're a day late and a dollar short, pal!" He stalked back to his cubicle, pulled his jacket on, strode down the main aisle, and went through the doors to the elevator area. That was the last we ever saw of him. On Friday, we learned that Derrick had been reassigned to another project.

***

About nine months later, I dropped into the Golden Duck to pick up a carryout on a snowy Friday evening. As usual, the waiting area of the take-out-only restaurant was overcrowded with hungry hipsters waiting in line to pick up their orders. As I stamped the snow off of my shoes, shrugged off the cold, and started getting used to the relative warmth of the waiting area, I slowly became aware of the man in line directly ahead of me. He had on well-worn loafers and faded jeans, and his long blond hair flowed over the collar of his black pea coat. When he turned his head slightly to the right, I caught part of his profile. It was Jim. I guess that even sociopaths like Peking duck.

Jim continued to turn his head farther to the right, and I realized that he might soon see me in his peripheral vision. I quickly shuffled two steps to his left so that I was out of sight behind him on his left-hand side. I must have done it too quickly because he reacted swiftly. He turned his entire body 180 degrees to his left in a quick motion. I was suddenly locked in the gaze of those pitiless blue eyes.

"Well, hello," he said and smiled. It was the first time I had ever seen him smile, and I was relieved to notice that he did not have pointed teeth.

"Hey, there." I replied. I looked away in an effort to indicate that we were only going to exchange "hellos." But, being socially agnostic, Jim didn't pick up on my signal. He continued to stare.

"Um, so where are you working now?" I asked, breaking down under his visual assault.

"I have a gig at another insurance company," he said, without giving the name of the company. "And you?"

"Mark and I are working on a three-month gig at a bank now," I said. If he wasn't going to name names, neither was I.

"Hmmm . . . ," said Jim. "I'd like to introduce you to my girlfriend. This is Lissette."

A petite woman in jeans with a white faux-rabbit fur coat and a mountain of wildly tossed, curly brunette hair turned around to face me. She had a devastatingly attractive face with a thin nose, high cheekbones, a pointed chin, and deeply red lips. She was wearing sunglasses. Sunglasses? It was nighttime.

There was no way that a guy like Jim should have had such a knockout for a girlfriend. So, I vaguely wondered if maybe he was some sort of Svengali and she was under his control. I resisted the urge to yell, "*Run, I'll call the police!*" Instead, I said, "I'm Michael. Pleased to meet you."

"Likewise," she said with a slight smile. We shook hands.

"Um, are you a programmer too?" I asked.

"No," she said. "I'm a psychiatrist."

Oh, so that's how it was. She was probably his handler, the one person in the world who kept him tethered to the rest of humanity.

A gap formed in the line behind where Jim and Lissette were standing as patrons' orders were fulfilled at the counter, they left, and the rest of the line moved forward. I pointedly looked at the gap, both because I was hungry and because it was socially awkward considering the long line behind us. Jim didn't get the gesture, but Lissette did. She turned, saw the gap, took Jim's elbow, and moved him backwards two big steps.

Jim continued to stare at me as if he were about to say something. But, he did not.

"Um, I guess that you don't miss Derrick," I offered, trying to fill the awkward silence.

"Derrick . . ." Jim said. "Yeah, Derrick . . ." he trailed off with what looked like a gleam in his impenetrable blue eyes. "I took care of Derrick," he said.

"Took care of him," I repeated. I had vague visions of Derrick's body occupying multiple black plastic trash bags in some landfill on the edge of town. Not wanting to be an accessory after the fact, but still very curious, I asked, "Took care of him . . . how?"

"Well, you see, Derrick finally crossed the line in one of those Monday status meetings. He mouthed off as usual, but this time he directed it at *me*." Jim smiled in remembrance.

"Something had to be done about him. So, I had Lissette call him up and say that she was a corporate recruiter working in the headquarters offices of Consolidated Physicians Associates Services, Inc. She told him that they had heard about his programming skills and technical savvy from many other people and that they had a great position for him," Jim continued. "She said that they were willing to give him a 20 percent raise and make him a project leader."

Consolidated Physician Associates Services, Inc., was a medium-sized HMO with its headquarters located in the city. They ran dozens of health clinics throughout the state and were actually my own medical services provider.

I glanced back at Lissette. She continued to smile thinly from beneath her dark sunglasses.

"Wasn't he at all suspicious?" I asked.

"No," said Lissette. "I know the personality type. I played to his ego using flattery. It was easy."

"I arranged for Derrick to go to one of Consolidated Physicians Associates Services' clinics on the fifteenth story of the Baxter Building for an interview on a Friday afternoon. I told him it was a headquarters branch office. Then I called that clinic location and made an appointment for Derrick to see a doctor specializing in sexually transmitted diseases." She moved Jim back two more paces to account for a new gap in the line.

"What?" I sputtered. I didn't know whether to be distressed or to be amused.

"Yes, so Derrick was expecting a meeting with a corporate recruiter at that address. And the clinic was expecting Derrick to show up for an exam. I called him the Thursday before the meeting to go over a checklist of things they would need: his résumé, three personal references, etc."

"Oh my God," I thought to myself, *"she's just as twisted as he is. They're a perfect pair."*

"Wow," I said, half in alarm, half in admiration, " . . . wow!"

"We will never really know what happened when he showed up at the clinic," said Lissette. "But he would have arrived at the correct address to a business with the same name as he was expecting. Once inside, he would have found out that he had an appointment. But it wasn't the kind of appointment he had been expecting."

"Man," I said, "I can't believe that you really did that." It was wicked, cruel, malicious, spiteful, and possibly criminal. It was also deeply, terribly, horribly funny.

"Yes," said Lissette, "we really did that." A large, sinister smile suddenly filled her entire face. When she smiled, her sunglasses slipped partway down her nose, revealing two disturbingly fathomless black eyes that locked onto me with twin thousand-yard stares.

"I guess that he's the one who ended up . . . ," and then her voice dropped down two octaves into a perfect imitation of Derrick's deep, gravelly voice ". . . a day late and a dollar short, pal!"

0100 PLAYING FOOTSIE

The *Consultant's Room* was actually a pretty nice workspace. It was a brightly lit, 36-by-36-foot room with rows of desks along three of the walls and a very long table in the middle. Each desk faced the wall and had a writing surface, drawers, a filing cabinet, an overhead bin, and privacy walls so that you did not see the neighbor on either side unless you pushed your chair a couple of feet backwards. The long table in the middle of the room had a row of five work areas on two of its sides. Each work area had a computer monitor, some desk space on either side of the keyboard, and a two-foot-high divider to keep your work private from your neighbors' work.

Some computer monitors were connected to the mainframe computers; others, to the UNIX servers. There were usually two of us working on the terminals tied to the mainframe and four others working on the UNIX terminals. Though we shared the same workspace, we had a friendly rivalry going on between us. We mainframers thought that the UNIX systems were primitive and unsophisticated. The UNIX programmers thought the mainframe systems were overly complicated and that *real programmers* only programmed under UNIX. No doubt, both groups were right and both groups were wrong.

Mid-morning on my first week there, I was engrossed in writing a program on the mainframe when the four UNIX programmers suddenly exploded with startled oaths. They looked at each other, swore, tossed pens down onto their desks in anger, and left the room muttering. The UNIX system had gone down.

I sat there for a minute with smug thoughts about how mainframe computers were far more reliable than UNIX systems. However, these thoughts quickly evaporated when I realized that the thing deep under the table that my right foot had been playing with all morning long was actually a thick power cord. The cord was attached to the controller unit that connected the UNIX terminals to the UNIX server. I had slowly but surely worked the cord out of the electrical socket and brought the controller down.

It took only seconds for me to dive beneath the table and apply the proper corrective maintenance. Once it was plugged back in, the controller rebooted itself with a whir and a flash of LED lights. The UNIX programmers returned minutes later with cups of coffee and the UNIX system administrator. They all had puzzled expressions on their faces when they saw that the system was back up and running. I decided not to burden them with lengthy explanations. Instead, I concentrated on my work and sat with my feet planted flat and firm under my chair.

0101 THE BUGSOUT OPTION

It would not be very nice to call Henry a *kiss ass*. Not very nice, but very accurate. Henry was a kiss ass, a suck-up, a toady, a brown nose, a yes man, an apple polisher, a boot licker, a backslapper, a fawner, a doter, a flatterer, and a lackey all packaged into one very annoying, *I incessantly need to impress the boss*, junior programmer. He was constantly in the project manager's cubicle, loudly bragging to Corbin about some programming technique that he had just used or some programming language construct that he had just found out about. The only thing that put him on our radar screen—the only thing that annoyed us to the point where we simply couldn't ignore him—was that he was constantly sidling up to us and prodding us for new information that he could use to impress Corbin.

Mark and I were experienced mid-level programmers who worked for a small consulting company. We were assigned to work on a large development project at a Fortune 100 company located downtown. There was an even mix of programmers from our company and programmers from the client firm. Mark and I had worked together on a previous consulting gig, so we tended to hang out with one another.

One day, Henry came over to Mark's cubicle.

"Hey Mark, got a second?" Henry asked.

"Henry, I'm really pretty busy," Mark replied, not bothering to look up.

"I know, but I could really use some help with a couple of my programs," Henry pressed. "They are supposed to create the credit balance reports, but I can't even get them to compile correctly."

"I'm under deadline pressure," Mark said. "I've got to get this program done before I leave tonight."

"What about you?" Henry asked me. I had made the mistake of looking up, and he had caught me.

"Same thing as Mark," I replied. "We all have to get these programs done before tomorrow's integrated system test."

"Sure," said Henry, clearly deflated. Then, under his breath as he walked away: "What the hell good is it to have so-called *consultants* if they can't help you out when you need them."

I did a slow burn when I heard that comment and looked over at Mark. He looked back at me, and I could see that he was also irked.

"I'm getting pretty tired of that guy," Mark said. "He's

constantly coming to us looking for help, gets it, and then runs off to Corbin to tell him how clever *he* is with what *we* show him. That's it. I am not going to help him anymore."

"Well, you know that's going to be a problem," I said. "We tried that approach a few weeks ago, and he went running to Corbin saying that we were not sharing information with him. You remember that Corbin told us that part of our job here as consultants is to help his junior staff. Henry is going to go back and cry to Corbin again."

"Mmm . . . ," said Mark. "You're right, but I am sick of him bugging us about his buggy programming."

That's when I got a nasty idea. I told Mark about it. He loved it, and we decided that we would do it after we had completed the *must-get-done* programs we were working on that day.

Unfortunately, our real-life programming work took much longer than we had anticipated. I made a run for sub sandwiches, chips, and sodas sometime around six-thirty. We ended up working on our respective programs until about nine o'clock. But even though both of us were totally buzzed with fatigue, neither of us wanted to leave until we had put our plan into motion.

"Ready?" I asked Mark.

"Ready!" he replied. Mark rolled his swivel chair across the aisle to my cubicle, and we began.

We opened the directory where Henry's programs were stored. We sorted them into order, from most recently modified to least recently modified. I opened the most recently modified program, and we started browsing it together.

"Oh my God," Mark exclaimed, saying aloud what the two of us were thinking, "this is godawful!"

Henry's program was a mishmash of twisted logic, tortured program flow, and badly named variables. It meandered in many different directions and did numerous unnecessary operations before heading towards the true purpose that it was intended for. It was indeed *godawful*!

"You sure you *really* want to do this?" Mark asked.

"Yeah. It's going to be a lot of work, but it will be totally worth it," I replied. "I'll take this one; you take the next one."

Mark grunted his agreement, wheeled his chair back to his cubicle, and went to work. I could hear his keys clicking away, and his occasional groans when he hit a particularly bad piece of twisted logic or a very poorly formed program construct.

It took us about two hours to get both programs cleaned up. First, we fixed the many programming language syntax errors in Henry's code so that the programs compiled cleanly — that is, the compiler found no syntax errors and turned the source code into machine-readable code that could be executed on the server. Then we fixed the logic errors so that the programs produced reasonable facsimiles of the required reports. When we were done, we were even more exhausted than after we had been working on our own programs. Nonetheless, we parted company in good spirits, full of anticipation on how things might play out.

The next morning, Mark caught Henry as he walked by our cubicles on his way into the office.

"Hey Henry, got a minute?" he called out.

"What do *you* want?" Henry asked petulantly. "I thought that you were too busy to talk to your fellow programmers."

"Sorry to give you that impression," said Mark glibly. "I was really busy yesterday and had to get my program ready for today's integrated system test. I didn't mean to be short with you."

"A lot of good that does me now," Henry whined. "My programs aren't ready for the system test. I could have used your help yesterday."

"Not a problem," said Mark. "I can help you now."

"But the integrated systems test starts in about 30 minutes," said Henry. "I was on my way to tell Corbin that my stuff isn't ready and we needed to postpone the test."

"Not necessary," said Mark. "We can get the bugs out of your program in a flash. Have you ever heard of the BUGSOUT option?"

Though Henry was a pretty inexperienced programmer, his pride never allowed him to say that he didn't know anything outright. So, his reply did not surprise us.

"Yes, I did hear about that option. But that was a long time ago. Can you refresh my memory?"

"Sure," said Mark. "But I am surprised that you have heard about it since it is an undocumented feature not found in any of the programming manuals. It is a very powerful facility that is only known to and used by very experienced consultants."

Henry beamed at the idea that Mark thought he was one of the cognoscenti.

"Yes, I've heard all of that, too," Henry lied. "But remind me again how it works."

"It's simple," Mark explained. "You type BUGSOUT—all in caps—in a comment block at the very top of your program. It has to be the very first thing in the program. Then compile and run the program. All of the bugs will be removed, and your program will produce output. It's that simple."

A dubious expression played across Henry's face. "But how is that possible?" he asked suspiciously.

"It's pretty straightforward," said Mark, selling the idea. "The compiler has an *expert system* built into it. As you know, an expert system is composed of two major components: a knowledge base and an inference engine. The compiler's initial knowledge base gets bigger and bigger as more and more programmers submit erroneous programs for compilation and then correct them. The knowledge base records all of the programming mistakes and how they were corrected. The inference engine uses heuristic techniques to sift through the knowledge base and substitute the correct code for syntactical errors and logic mistakes."

Henry had been nodding his head knowingly during Mark's explanation. "Ah, I thought it was something like that," he said. "How do you trigger *bugs out*, again?"

"It's easy," said Mark. "You type BUGSOUT—all one word—in a comment block at the very top of your program. But make sure that BUGSOUT is specified in all capital letters."

"BUGSOUT. One word. All caps. Comment block. Top of

program," Henry repeated, taking mental notes. "Thanks, I'll give it a try."

Henry started to leave.

"Wait," said Mark, "let's do it here. Pull up a chair."

Henry pulled up a chair and sat down next to Mark. I walked over and hovered behind them.

"All right, where are your programs located?" asked Mark.

Henry told Mark which directory the programs were stored in, and Mark pointed and clicked his way to them. He opened the first program and began typing. He typed BUGSOUT in a comment block at the top of the program. He set the program up for compilation and fired it off. A few moments later, the compilation completed successfully with absolutely no errors.

"Wow!" Henry exclaimed. "I had all kinds of problems with that program yesterday. That *is* powerful!"

"You haven't seen anything yet," Mark said. He ran the program.

The program ran without errors and produced a report. Mark opened the report.

"Amazing!" Henry yelped. "Yesterday, I barely had the report logic figured out. I can't believe how good BUGSOUT really is."

"Why do you think we consultants make the big bucks?" Mark asked him with a conspiratorial smile.

"Uh, gotta go!" Henry said suddenly. "I've got to fix my other program before the integrated systems test."

Without a *thank you* or any acknowledgment of appreciation, Henry took off for his own cubicle.

Moments later, we heard Henry's squeals of delight when his other program compiled correctly and then when it produced its requisite report. Mark and I had a good silent laugh together. Then we got back to our serious programming work, though both of us would suddenly burst out with an uncaptured guffaw whenever we thought of our little joke.

Later that morning, the entire project team was in the conference room for a debriefing to discuss *lessons learned* from the integrated systems test. Mark and I could see Henry eagerly looking around the room and being much more animated than usual. As the meeting wound down, we found out why.

"Henry asked me if he could say a few words at the end of today's meeting," Corbin said. "Henry?"

Henry took a sheaf of papers from a folder sitting near his notebook and passed it around the room. When I got my copy, I almost lost it. There on the paper was the word BUGSOUT in a comment block. I looked across the table at Mark who had just received his handout. He sputtered, but quickly caught himself. He avoided making eye contact with me because he knew that would set him off, big time.

"The handout I am distributing has a very powerful, undocumented programming feature that can be very important to each programmer sitting in this room," Henry proudly pontificated.

"The BUGSOUT option is only known to a handful of clever programmers. You code it in a comment block at the top of your program, and it debugs the program. It uses an expert system with a knowledge base, an inference engine, and heuristic techniques. I've used it on some of my programs for this project," concluded Henry with a smug, proud, knowing smile.

I slowly scanned the faces of the experienced programmers who were sitting around the table. Their expressions ranged from disinterest to amusement to outright disbelief. The room was silent. Henry's smug smile froze on his face as he also perused the faces of his teammates. The room was silent some more. Finally, Chen dismissively tossed his copy of the handout down on the table in front of him.

"Doesn't work," he said.

"Yes, it does," said Henry, "I've used it myself."

"No way," said Chen. "Nothing in a comment block gets executed. You should know that."

"But the BUGSOUT option does work," said Henry. "I've seen it for myself."

"Not possible," chimed in Naomi, closing her notebook and capping her pen. "I've been programming in this language for fifteen years and never heard of it."

"BUGSOUT," urged Henry, pointing to a copy of his handout, "The BUGSOUT option!"

"Preposterous," said Tim, starting to rise. "There is no such thing."

"No, BUGSOUT *does* exist! It really does work," bleated Henry with panic in his eyes and in his voice as his big moment slowly slipped away. "I've seen how powerful it is—how much good it can do!"

He turned to Mark.

"Help me out here, Mark. Tell them about BUGSOUT," pleaded Henry.

The conference room suddenly got quiet as people in various states of packing up or of walking out stopped to listen. Mark was a very respected programmer, and they all wanted to hear what he had to say.

Mark paused for about thirty seconds, looking down at the conference table with a deep, thoughtful expression on his face. Suddenly, his eyes brightened as if he had had a sudden realization, and he looked up at Henry. Henry looked relieved and started to smile.

"Nope," Mark said, shaking his head, "I'm afraid I don't have any idea what you are talking about."

0110 I SMELL A RAT

It was the headquarters complex of an established paper product manufacturing company, and everything about the place was oppressive, dirty, and worn. The multi-acre site was surrounded by a rusting, eight-foot-high chain-link fence topped with both barbed wire and razor wire. It was hard to tell how effective the fence was at keeping people out. But judging from the buildup along the fence line, it excelled at keeping plastic bags, dried leaves, paper coffee cups, and other urban debris from trespassing.

You entered the football-field-sized parking lot through a guard post manned by hardened, unsmiling, officious guards dressed in uniforms styled somewhere between the garb of state police and that of mall cops. The guards subjected visitors to a series of stern questions and very careful ID checks before calling the main building for verification that they were expected. Then they filled out temporary parking passes and barked out a series of complicated directions to exactly where visitors were supposed to park. *C'mon folks, this is a paper manufacturing plant, not the Pentagon.*

The vast parking lot was a labyrinth of one-way lanes with small-sized parking slots marked by divider lines so faded that you were not sure if you were parking correctly unless you eased in between two already-parked cars. The lot was organized into large overlapping parking zones and forested with scores of signs. Plant Employee Parking Only. Office Employee Parking Only. Two-hour Visitor Parking Only. Employee Pickup Parking Only. Temporary Parking Only. Blue Pass Parking Only. Overflow Parking Only. *Violators Will Be Towed at Their Own Risk and Expense!*

At one end of the parking lot sat the manufacturing plant, an enormous, sprawling three-story building that constantly spewed steam, smoke, and *who knows what* into the crisp New England air. *EPA? We don't need no stinking EPA!*

At the other end of the parking lot sat the corporate headquarters building, a long, brown, soulless two-story structure that must have been architecturally out of date the moment it was completed back in the1960s. The reddish-brown stains that dripped down the sides of the edifice from each of the rusting window fixtures made the building look like it was crying. *Abandon all hope ye who enter here.*

The Data Processing Department was on the second floor of the office building in a vast room divided into gray-walled, metal-sided cubicles. Each cubicle contained an ancient metal desk, a heavy metal swivel chair, a big metal filing cabinet, and a freestanding metal coat rack. The cubicle walls were shoulder-high so that you could not see your neighbor's workspace when you were sitting down. The office was deathly quiet with almost no conversations taking place in the cubicle passageways. People talked in hushed tones on the telephone and in muted tones when visiting a colleague's cubicle. Something about that place either invited silence or demanded it. Likely the latter.

I was hired to work on a three-month programming project with several other computer consultants in the office building. On my first day, I passed the parking lot guard's officious interrogation and was granted a parking pass. After 10 minutes of driving around the lot interpreting the various signs, I parked in what I believed was a valid parking spot for a visiting consultant. I walked into the visitor's lobby where another squad of humorless guards was waiting to ask me some questions, check my ID, and allow me to fill out a guest entry form. Then I was permitted to go up to the second floor to meet Tony, my organization's lead consultant at the site.

Tony met me at the top of the stairwell and led me through the maze of cubicles. He introduced me to the other people from our company and to several of the organization's programmers whom I would be working with. Tony dropped me off at my own cheerless, well-worn cubicle and told me to settle in. He returned moments later with reams of project documentation and programming specifications. My first assignment was to read through the material and become familiar with the flow of the many interrelated computer programs that made up the system.

In the afternoon, Tony stopped by again and gave me a three-ring binder filled with programs for me to review to get up to speed with what had already been programmed. The programs were annotated with yellow sticky notes where the changes would likely have to be made. The firm's security guy also came by and had me fill out forms to get my user ID and password in order to access the computer system. He gave me a stapled handout on how to log into the mainframe computer and a must-read booklet on corporate system security practices.

At the end of the day, I scooped up all of the paperwork on my desk, stuffed it into my briefcase, and took it home with me. I wanted to be prepared to hit the ground running the next day when the security work was completed and I was given access to the computer system. It would give me a leg up on the programming requirements and help me to meet the strict deadlines we were facing. After dinner, I studied the documentation, the specs, and the programs late into the night.

About ten o'clock the next day, the security guy showed up at the door to my cubicle and asked me to come with him. He marched me past rows of quiet, heads-down programmers to a meeting room at the far end of the cubicle farm. Tony and the project manager were both sitting in the room looking serious. I was asked to sit down, and the security guy closed the door behind me.

"We have a report that you were seen taking documents from the premises," the manager stated.

"Oh, right. I took some documentation and programs home to study last night," I replied. Oh, so *that* was what this was all about.

"*Study?*" he asked skeptically.

"Yes, I usually do that when I get to a new assignment. I like to come up to speed fast so that I can be effective as soon as possible."

"And you actually take work home to *study* it?" he asked skeptically.

"Well, yes, I do," I replied.

"Did you show the documentation and programs to anybody else?" asked the security guy.

"No, of course not. Who would I show them to?"

"Are you married?" asked the security guy in a tone that showed he was pleased with such an insightful question.

"Yes, I am. But my wife wouldn't be interested in that material," I answered, starting to get annoyed.

"And what does she do?" he pressed.

"She is an elementary school teacher," I replied. I could see the disappointment in his eyes.

"And you didn't show the material to anybody else? Nobody asked to see the material you took from here, right?" asked the manger.

"No, nobody else!" I replied hotly.

They all exchanged glances, and I could see that they were satisfied.

"Okay, we are done here. You can go back to your cubicle," the manager said.

I left the conference room, trekked back to my cubicle, and just sat there steaming mad. I slowly rotated my chair a full 360-degrees looking at the view from my desk. From my sitting position, there did not appear to be any way that somebody could see my desk directly. Yet somebody had seen me put the papers into my briefcase.

I wondered who it could have been. Was it the poker-faced male programmer with thinning, slicked-back, 1950s-style hair who sat in the cubicle to my left? Could it be the eyes-down, sad-looking woman programmer who sat in the cubicle to my right? Or perhaps it was the grizzled, sweater-vested older male programmer who sat on the other side of the cubicle wall directly ahead of me? But the only way for one of them to have had me in their line of sight would have been if they had been standing while I was packing up. I think that I would have noticed one of them staring over the cubicle wall at me. But even if they had been standing, why would they have thought my actions were suspicious enough to have warranted reporting me to the "authorities"?

Tony and the security guy dropped by my cubicle half an hour after my interrogation. They told me that my explanation had been judged acceptable, and the security guy told me that I would get my computer access later that day. I was told that I could never, ever take any programs or documentation home. And I was to never, ever bring my briefcase back into the building. I seriously thought about telling them to take the job and shove it. But I was an independent consultant and really needed the paycheck. So, pushing back my annoyance and anger, I said, "Yes, that will never happen again."

Two mornings later, I was in the middle of modifying a program when suddenly my workstation flickered off, as did the lights and the building's air-conditioning unit. The whole floor was plunged into twilight and an eerie silence. After a few minutes, the silence was broken by the murmuring sounds of dozens of low conversations. I stood up to look around and saw that everybody else was standing up and looking around. There was confusion, anxiety, and even a little fear in the faces that surrounded me. Somebody came up from the first floor and said that the power was off in the entire office building as well as in the plant on the other side of the parking lot.

At 12:30 word came down that the source of the problem was still under investigation and that power was not expected to be restored for the rest of the day. We could all go home. The news produced a carnival-like atmosphere in that grim office space. I could not believe that I actually saw the firm's employees smiling and heard them laughing and talking at normal volume levels as they filed out of the building and into the parking lot.

The next morning, the power was back on, and the office had its usual somber demeanor. It turned out that the problem had occurred in the manufacturing plant. A rat had chewed through a major cable, electrocuting itself and shorting out the transformer that provided power to both the plant and the office complex. A repair crew had worked through the night to remove the toasted rat, clean out the many rats' nests they discovered around the plant's main electrical equipment, replace the transformer, and restore power to both the plant and the office complex.

A rat! The entire organization was taken down for a day by a rat. How appropriate. That place had rats all right—both of the animal and of the human kind!

0111 AND THEN THERE WERE NONE

A co-worker of mine once worked for a company where the entire Telecommunications Department was suddenly wiped out.

Downsizing? No.

Outsourcing? No.

Mass resignations? Certainly not!

Greed? Yes.

Dishonesty? Yes.

Stupidity? Certainly so!

It happened over a two-week period. Although nobody was physically hurt, the entire organization suffered for many months until replacements could be hired, trained, and brought up to speed on the work.

The Telecommunications Department at this medium-sized

Fortune 500 company was composed of three people: the Director, the Manager, and the Person Who Really Did All of the Work. One day, the Manager wandered into the Director's office while the Director was out to lunch. He happened to see a copy of the travel reimbursement form for the Director's latest business trip lying on the desk. The Manager picked it up and read through it. Somehow, he realized that the Director had been cheating on his travel expenses. They had never really gotten along very well, so the Manager decided to use this information to his advantage.

Later that afternoon, he walked into the Director's office and told him what he had found out. He said that he would forget all about the travel expense discrepancies if the Director would give him an out-of-sequence raise. Since they did not get along, the Director told him where to go and threw him out of his office.

The Manager went directly to the Personnel Department, gave them a photocopy of the reimbursement form that he had made, and explained how the Director had cheated on it. Then he returned to his office and contemplated how he would spend his big raise when his boss was fired and he was promoted to Director.

This particular organization was very concerned about its corporate public image and had very rigid personal integrity policies. Accordingly, the Personnel Department launched an internal investigation of the entire Telecommunications Department. They determined that the Director had indeed cheated on his travel expense report and on other expense reports over several years time. Consequently, they summoned him down to the Personnel Department and confronted him with the evidence they had gathered. He had no good explanation for his many accounting "mistakes" on business trip expenses for the past several years and admitted his malfeasance. So, they fired him.

And then there were two.

The Manager was elated when he learned that the Director had been fired. He was delighted when he got his call to come down to the Personnel Department. He went there envisioning exactly what he would say when he was asked if he would take the job as Director of Telecommunications. When he entered the offices, he was met with a group of serious, stony-faced corporate personnel officers. The Personnel Department had launched a very thorough investigation into all facets of the Telecommunications Department. They had discovered that, amazingly enough, the Manager had also been cheating the company on *his* travel expenses, too. So, they fired the Manager on the spot.

And then there was one.

The Personnel Department sent for the Person Who Really Did All of the Work. When the Person Who Really Did All of the Work got his call to come down to the Personnel Department, he was happy. He had been alarmed by the firing of the Director and the Manager. But since he did not travel and had not cheated on expense reports, he was not overly concerned. He envisioned being promoted to manager and getting somebody else to do all of the work.

However, things were not quite that simple. The Person Who Really Did All of the Work had two computers in his office—one for normal office work and one for directly monitoring the company's telecommunications equipment. Since he was on call and fielded many problems from home during evening hours and on weekends, he had asked the Manager if he could swap his smaller, at-home computer monitor with the larger monitor from his normal office work computer. This gave him a larger monitor screen at home, which was easier on his eyes. The Manager told him that it was okay, as long as he ultimately returned it. However, there was no written record of this agreement, and the Manager who had been fired now refused to talk to anybody at the company. Since taking office equipment home without permission was against corporate policy, the Personnel Department relieved the final member of the Telecommunications Department of his duties.

And then there were none.

1000 MOTORCYCLE MAMA

I don't know what Jimmy's official job title was, but it might as well have been *Chief Office Annoyer*. He was one of those people who rubbed everybody the wrong way. In his case, it wasn't accidental. Jimmy went out of his way to bug people and seemed to relish the negative feedback he got from his many daily encounters. Though he flaunted the common laws of social discourse and comportment that the rest of us operated under, he never seemed to get into trouble. Maybe he had an upper management connection that protected him. Perhaps people were so used to antics that they largely ignored them. Or maybe everybody else thought that he was funny, and I was the one person whose nerves he grated on. Whatever the case, Jimmy seemed to get away with murder in an otherwise serious business environment.

Jimmy was a doughy twenty-something with unkempt mousy brown hair and at least two days of beard growth. In an office where business formal and business casual dress were the norm, he wore jeans and a pullover sports jersey featuring his favorite team of the day. He would whistle one of the two main Star Wars themes loudly to himself, so we always knew when he had arrived at the entrance to our office area. If you were unfortunate enough to be nearby, he would chat you up in a one-sided conversation in a *way-too-loud-for-the-office* voice. Jimmy would talk at you about everything under the sun from sports to movies to pop culture; whatever seemed to pop into his mind on that particular day was fair game. He didn't pause during his *conversation*s, so there was no easy way to disengage. You would have to forcefully interrupt by saying something like "I've got to go," turn, and walk away. And when you did, Jimmy would continue talking to you behind your back the whole time that you hurried away.

Jimmy's most aggravating trait was that he would come up with his own name for you and then call it out, loudly, whenever he saw you. For instance, he somehow found out that I was a serious runner. So, whenever he would see me, he would yell out, "Runner Man!" or "Hey, Runner Man!" or "There goes *the* Runner Man!" It didn't matter that we were in a quiet office environment where people were concentrating on writing computer programs or talking to clients on the phone. We could hear him hail somebody by their nickname across the entire office area. I often saw other people roll their eyes and shake their heads at his loud comments. But I never heard anybody complain.

As far as I could tell, Jimmy had two jobs. First, he delivered the interoffice and postal mail to our mailbox cubbies in the rack just within the entrance to our cubicle farm. Second, he delivered the mainframe printouts to a wall-hanging file-folder rack that also sat just within the entrance to our office. Consequently,

Jimmy visited our area several times each day during the normal course of his duties. He would come in with his load in a satchel, dump the mail or printouts out on the table, sort through them, and file them as appropriate.

One day, my neighbor Wendy and I were talking over the cubicle wall.

"Did you hear what happened to Jimmy?" she asked.

"No, what?" I wanted to know.

"He got into trouble. He was disciplined for calling the courier a name," she explained. "You know that good-looking guy in motorcycle leathers who delivers special packages?"

I knew exactly who she was talking about. From time to time, we would see a guy come into the office area to deliver special packages for a courier service. He was stunningly handsome with well-styled brown hair, a thin beard, and wolfish facial features. He wore brown motorcycle leathers from head to toe and stylish motorcycle boots. He always moved quickly and had a serious, no-nonsense look on his face.

"What happened?" I asked.

"Well, it seems that Jimmy saw the guy and called out 'Motorcycle Mama.' Apparently, the first time he did it, the guy ignored him. He did it again when the guy returned a few days later. The courier confronted him and told him to shut up and not to bother him. Of course, Jimmy being Jimmy he just couldn't help himself. So, as the guy was leaving, he yelled out something like 'Bye, bye Motorcycle Mama.'"

"Wow," I said. "That guy is scary, I wouldn't mess with him."

"Right," said Wendy. "The guy exploded on Jimmy and cursed him out. He went to Jimmy's manager and complained. He said that he had a job to do and that Jimmy was interfering with it. He told the manger that he had warned Jimmy, but Jimmy had persisted. He demanded to know what the manger was going to do about the situation."

"Poor Jimmy," I smiled.

"Yeah, poor Jimmy," Wendy laughed. "So, Jimmy was called into the office and made to apologize to the guy. He is under strict orders to never say anything to him ever again. Or else . . ."

That is when I got a nasty idea. I thought about all of the times that Jimmy had corralled me into one of his idiotic, one-way conversations. I thought of all of the times I had disengaged only to have him talking to me as I hurried away. I thought about all of the times that he had greeted me or called after me "Runner Man!" or "Hey, Runner Man!" or "There goes *the* Runner Man!" And I knew that I was going to go through with my nasty idea.

My idea involved the mainframe printouts that Jimmy delivered. The mainframe printouts were on *green bar* paper that was 14 and 7/8 inches wide by 11 inches long. Each printout had the last name of the person who had submitted the computer program for execution in big block letters on the first page. When Jimmy dumped the printouts on the table, he sorted through them and put them into the file rack folder in alphabetic order according to last name. Thereafter, we would drop by the rack and pick up our printouts—me from the folder bin labeled "R."

Because I was in the Systems Programming Group, I had a pretty good idea of how I could submit a batch job to run on the mainframe anonymously. So, I sat down and crafted an IEFBR14 utility that did pretty much nothing except "touch" a data set that many people had access to. I modified the Job Control Language (JCL) so that the batch job would print out "MOTORCYCLE MAMA" on the banner page. Once it was ready, I submitted the batch job that would execute the IEFBR14 utility and produce the printout. Then I deleted the program to cover my tracks and waited to see what would transpire.

The fireworks happened after lunchtime. Jimmy's irritating whistling cut through my concentration as I sat immersed in writing a SAS program. I eased upward out of my chair and peeked over the cubicle wall. Across the office area, I could see Jimmy dump his satchel of green bar printouts onto the table and begin sorting. I sat down so that I wouldn't attract his attention. I waited. I waited some more. Suddenly, there it was!

"Motorcycle Mama!" Jimmy exclaimed loudly enough for everybody to hear. "Motorcycle Mama? What the hell!"

I chanced a look over the top of my cubicle and saw that a half-dozen other people were doing the same.

"Who did this?" Jimmy yelled, looking across the room at the growing group of impromptu spectators. "Who did this? You think your funny, huh? Well, somebody's going pay! Somebody's going to get in trouble!"

Jimmy stomped out into the corridor with the printout in his hands. I guessed that he was going to complain to his manager. But I was not worried because I had covered my tracks pretty well. There was nothing in that printout that could possibly point back to me. So, I sat in my cubicle laughing to myself and enjoying my little joke.

Unfortunately, my little joke did not last very long. Late in the afternoon, I got an email from Ron, the manager of the Systems Programming Group. The message said that a batch job had been submitted at 10:43 that morning with a specific JES 2 (Job Entry Subsystem 2) number, which he provided in the email. Since I was the organization's Computer Performance Analyst and had access to the IBM Systems Management Facility (SMF), which records—among many, many other things—information about the who, what, when, and where of batch jobs, he wanted me to determine who had submitted that particular job for execution. The email said that this was a sensitive, private matter, and that Ron wanted me to be discrete. He instructed me to bring the *user ID* of who had submitted that batch job to him in the morning. Since our user IDs were composed of the first seven characters of our last name and our first initial, it was obvious what I would be reporting to Ron: RAITHELM.

I was trapped, and my little joke suddenly did not seem very funny anymore. There was only one thing for me to do. Feeling like a condemned man, I got up from my cubicle, walked down to Ron's office, and knocked on the door. Ron looked up and motioned me in. I closed the door behind me, and he looked at me quizzically.

"Yes?" Ron asked.

"Um . . . I know who submitted the job with the MOTORCYCLE MAMA banner page," I said.

"How could you?" asked Ron. "The SMF tapes don't roll over until after midnight. You can't run an analysis until tomorrow morning."

"I know because . . . it was me," I said with real shame. Ron had always been very good to me, and I really felt like I had let him down with my bad behavior.

"What? Why?" he asked, clearly astounded. I had always been a straight shooter, and this was definitely coming out of left field.

"Well, Jimmy is just always . . . I mean, Jimmy is just . . . such a . . . such a . . . *dick*!" I concluded honestly, suddenly finding the most descriptive word.

Ron stared at me hard for what seemed like an eternity. I squirmed under his gaze, wondering what my punishment would be. At the very least, I would owe Jimmy an apology. I would definitely get a letter of reprimand in my personnel file. It would probably negatively affect my next performance review and consequently my raise. I might be told to get counseling. I did not think that I would be fired, but you never knew.

Finally, Ron smiled. "Yes, Jimmy is definitely a *dick*," he said. "I understand that he gets under everybody's skin. But, you don't have to sink down to his level."

"No, I guess not," I replied sheepishly.

"Did you learn anything from this?" Ron asked.

"Yes, I did," I said.

"Will you ever do anything like this again?" he pressed.

"No. Never!" I replied, suddenly sensing salvation.

"Okay, then this matter is closed. I will tell Jimmy's manager that it has been taken care of internally, and that the guilty party has been severely reprimanded. There is no need to name names."

"Thank you very much, Ron," I said rising from the chair. "Believe me, I will never . . ."

"Dismissed!" he interrupted with a wave of his hand.

I bolted out of his office and headed towards the main throughway that led to my cubicle. Jimmy happened to be sorting through a batch of interoffice mail on the table near the door. As I walked by, he caught sight of me and belted out, "Hey, there goes the *Run-ner* Man!" I bristled at that and suddenly had a crazy urge to turn back on him and retort, "Hey, there goes the Motorcycle Mama!" But sanity and perhaps a little bit of maturity prevailed. Instead, I continued walking back to my cubicle where real work awaited me.

1001 THE BREAKFAST NOOK

At first, I thought that I was the only one who noticed it. But then fellow database administrator Rick casually mentioned that he had seen it on two occasions. And later a systems programmer named Steve remarked about finding it, too. Once the three of us realized that we were all tracking the same odd social anomaly, we made it our business to find out who the culprit was.

I was working in the Systems Group of a Fortune 100 company at the time. The company was renovating the section of the headquarters building we normally occupied, so they had moved us to a temporary office space several miles up the road. We shared a three-story building with a market research firm, a staffing placement company, an accounting partnership, several law offices, and a couple of medical practices. Our clean, modern, cubicle-farm office space was located on the second floor of the building. There was a break room with several tables, a coffee machine, and some vending machines that sold pastries and candy on the first floor. The bathrooms on all three floors were cleaned a couple of times a day, and there was ample free parking surrounding the building. All in all, it wasn't a bad environment to have to occupy for the nine months it would take to renovate our office space back at headquarters.

One morning, I went into a stall in the second-floor men's room and saw a used eight-ounce paper coffee cup and an empty chocolate cupcake wrapper sitting on the small metal shelf above the toilet paper holder. Somebody had actually eaten their breakfast in the men's room. *Are you kidding me?* I think that if I made a list of all of the places that I would *not* want to eat breakfast, a men's room toilet stall would be somewhere near the top of the list. But who could it have been—one of our own or one of the building's other occupants? I went about my business and forgot about it for a few days. Then another morning, I saw it again—an empty coffee cup and a chocolate cupcake wrapper in a different toilet stall in the same men's room. That got my curiosity going. So, every morning, I would surreptitiously check the three stalls in the men's room to see if the mystery breakfaster had been there. Some days I was rewarded with evidence of his morning repast, and many days I was not.

A few weeks after my initial discovery, Rick and I were having lunch in the break room and talking about the relative merits of the contents of the vending machines. That's when he mentioned having seen some of the wrappers from the chocolate cupcakes from one of the machines in the men's room along with paper cups from the coffee machine. The kicker was that he had seen them in a *first-floor* men's room. I told him about my sightings in the *second-floor* men's room. That's when Steve, who was sitting at an adjacent table, leaned in and told us he had noticed the same debris in both the second- and the third-floor men's rooms.

Steve came over to our table, and the three of us put our heads together to formulate a plan to track down the mystery loo diner. We all knew that whoever was having his *petit dejeuner* in the men's rooms was doing it before about 11:00 am in the morning when the building maintenance crew did their morning bathroom clean-up. None of us had ever seen the debris after the morning clean-up. So, we decided to split our resources and visit the bathrooms at random times between when we each got into the office and 11:00 am. Steve would take the third-floor men's room, I would take the second-floor men's room, and Rick would take the first-floor men's room. We would keep a spreadsheet with the dates and times that we found debris and also record whom we observed in or around the men's rooms at the time. Then we would try to correlate the comings and goings of the bathroom users with the left behind breakfast remains. That would lead to the determination of the mysterious men's room breakfast snacker's true identity.

Sounds relatively easy, right? Well, it wasn't. We were all pretty busy programmers, and it took some effort for us to remember to step away from our keyboards and sleuth out our assigned men's rooms with any regularity. We tried to be systematic, but our searches tended to be random, and—more often than not—tied to our own biological needs. Consequently, after about a month of "searching" and comparing notes, we were no closer to identifying our suspect than the day that each of us had first found his detritus.

Quite by chance, the mystery solved itself. Rick and I were walking down the hall one morning to head downstairs to the break room. Walking towards us from the direction of the second-floor men's room was Randolph, the natty Senior Director of the

Systems Group. Being our boss's boss, he was generally aloof to common members of the programming staff like us. But he had a special liking for Rick because they had both attended the same university. *Go Blue!* So, Randolph slowed down and smiled.

"Hey Rick, would you like some chocolate cupcakes?" Randolph asked stopping in front of us and holding up a package. "I put a dollar in the vending machine and two packages came out. I just ate the other one with my coffee and don't really want these."

"Thanks, Randolph," said Rick in a strained voice. He took the package of chocolate cupcakes.

"No problem," said Randolph. "Enjoy!" He continued down the hallway.

I looked at Rick. Rick looked back at me wide-eyed.

"You think so?" I asked.

"No way!" he said shaking his head from side to side.

We sprinted down the hall, past the stairwell entrance, and burst into the men's room. I hurried by the three urinals along the left-hand wall and turned into the first toilet stall with Rick hot on my heels. It was empty of debris.

"Nope!" I called out.

Rick pushed past me and into the second stall.

"Empty!" he called out.

I darted past Rick and zipped into the handicap stall at the end of the row. *Bingo!* There on top of the metal toilet paper holder sat a used eight-ounce paper coffee cup and an empty chocolate cupcake wrapper. Rick squeezed in besides me and looked at the trash.

"No way!" he gasped.

"Yes; it's true!" I replied.

So, it was Randolph. How improbable that was! The Ivy League–educated, articulate, immaculately dressed, very successful Senior Director of the Systems Group with the shiny BMW and the spotless office liked to eat his breakfasts in the men's room. Our boss's boss; the man who signed off on our reviews; the man who determined our raises; the man who made the ultimate decisions on our promotions—*he* was the clandestine bathroom breakfast snacker. Go figure!

When Rick and I got to the break room, we found Steve working on his laptop at one of the tables.

"What's up guys?" he asked. "Any progress on finding our Mystery Man?"

I looked at Rick. Rick looked back at me wide-eyed and surreptitiously shook his head from side to side to signal "no."

"What?" asked Steve, picking up on Rick's discomfort. "Did you guys have a breakthrough?"

"Um . . . no, not exactly." I said.

"Then, what?" Steve asked suspiciously. "You guys know *something*. What is it?"

"Well," I said. "Yes, we did learn something from Randolph,

just a few minutes ago."

Rick elbowed me in the ribs and barked out a desperate warning, "*Michael!*"

"What's that?" Steve asked.

"We learned that you can get two items for a dollar out of the center vending machine. You know, the one with the chocolate cupcakes."

Rick let out a heavy sigh of relief.

"No kidding?" Steve's eyes lit up.

Steve, Rick, and I each put a dollar into the center vending machine and each got two snack packages for the price of one. Steve sat back down at the table while Rick and I got ready to leave.

"By the way," I said, "Rick and I have decided that we are not really getting anywhere. So, we are calling off the search for the *Mystery Man*."

"Oh, okay," Steve said in a resigned tone. He tore open the cellophane wrapper of one of his packages of chocolate cupcakes and turned back to the program he was writing.

1010 WHAT GOES AROUND COMES AROUND

I had no idea that my entire world was about to be rocked when Jerry walked into my office area that day. I did not hear him enter the room because I was deep inside of a complex macro program that I was writing. I was in that sweet misty haze that envelops programmers who are hard at work—that cerebral, semi-sleep dream world landscaped with three-dimensional programming language statements, dancing data items, and endless streams of logic flows. When I finally realized that another human being had entered the room, I vaguely thought that it was one of my office mates. It wasn't until Jerry took hold of Arnold's swivel chair, rolled it up besides my desk, and said, "We've got to talk," that I realized my manager was in the room.

"Um . . . just a sec," I said trying to hold onto my train of thought. I finished typing the statement I was working on and pushed the *courtesy envelope* a bit by typing out two additional program statements that were in my head. Then I tabbed down several lines and put a comment in the program /* *Check status* *codes here */* so that I would be able to remember what needed to be done next.

"Yeah, what's up?" I asked. I was vaguely annoyed by the interruption, and I didn't try to hide it. Jerry was the on-site manager for our group of about 30 programming consultants. He was some sort of systems analyst, but the biggest part of his job was attending meetings with our clients to administer the contract. I only saw him when he collected my time sheet every two weeks or if there was some sort of administrative action that required my attention.

"Well, I'm afraid that I've got some bad news," he said. I saw an odd expression on his face. What was it? Frustration? Aggravation?

"What?" I asked with a bit of sarcasm. "Did I miscode one of the charging units on my time sheet, again?"

I saw a flash of hurt go across his face. "No, it's not that," Jerry said. And again he had that odd look. "It's just that . . . Well, I had a meeting with Anderson, Cahill, and the other client reps this afternoon. They requested a reduction in our contracting force for the upcoming fiscal year."

"Yeah, and . . . ?" I sighed heavily to show him that I didn't really care about his administrative work. It was after six in the evening on a Friday, almost everybody else had gone home for the weekend, the office area was nice and quiet. I wanted to get my program working correctly before going home, and here he was boring me with contract details. Wasn't that why they had invented email?

"And they want us to drop three positions from the contract," he continued.

All at once, I recognized the odd look on his face. It wasn't frustration. It wasn't aggravation. It was pity.

"Your position is one of the three that's going to be terminated."

"*My* position?" I was shocked. Five months earlier, I had left a stagnant but safe job at a very solid company for an opportunity with the consulting firm because it had offered a bit more pay and a bigger programming challenge. They were on year three of a seven-year contract with a major government agency, so the move had appeared to be pretty sound. I had received nothing but positive comments from my client contacts about the computer performance evaluation work that I had been doing since I got there. So, what the hell?

"Who else is being let go?" I asked. I guess that I wanted to know who else was expendable, who else was included on the list of the contract's flotsam and jetsam.

"Listen," said Jerry, "I am not supposed to talk about this to you or to the other two. Somebody from Corporate is going to call you in and discuss it with you. But I know that you have a wife and a kid—I do, too—and if it were me, I would want to know right away. That's why I am telling you. It's the right thing to do."

I realized that Jerry really was a good guy and that he was trying to help. No need to kill the messenger.

"How long do I have?" I asked.

"Well, the new fiscal year starts in about six weeks. The positions will be cut then."

"Okay, thanks for letting me know. I do appreciate it."

"You know . . . It is possible that Corporate can put you on another contract," Jerry said as he got up to leave. "Keep that in mind."

"Sure," I said. "I'll do that." But I knew that this contract offered the only fit they had with my particular skill set, which was analyzing the performance and capacity of mainframe computers. So, the thought was kind, but the point totally moot.

Anybody who has ever been laid off knows how tough it is to both digest the news and bring the news home. I was no exception. I racked my brain to try to figure out what I could have possibly done wrong and what I might have done better. But I couldn't come up with anything on either track. I had had a positive working relationship with my client contacts and had received some praise for my work every now and again. It was tough news to bring home late on a Friday night. But we were resilient. I spent the weekend gearing up for the job search ahead of me. I updated my résumé, combed through the want ads, and made a list of my industry contacts so that I could start networking. By Monday, I had a plan in place.

Corporate did not come up with a new position for me. But I did. Networking with industry friends and acquaintances, I was able to find a new job with another consulting company that had a solid contract at another federal facility. They did not know that I was desperate, so I was going to get a nice pay raise out of the move. Once I secured the new position, I gave my two-week's notice. Corporate did not seem surprised.

My workmates threw a goodbye luncheon for me at our

favorite Korean restaurant on my last day. There were about fifteen of us, evenly divided between consultants and our client co-workers. It was a pretty typical goodbye lunch with lots of laughter and recounting of work war stories over the kimchi and chimaek. The only thing that seemed a bit odd—especially in retrospect—was Phillip's behavior; he gave me peculiar long looks during the luncheon.

Phillip was the client organization's lead computer performance analyst. He had a few years less experience than I did and had come to me for advice on a number of occasions. He was sitting directly beside me to my right.

"What?" I asked him at one point when I turned to see him staring at me oddly, yet again.

"Nothing," he replied very defensively, turning away and digging into his bowl of jjajangmyeon.

I found out that it wasn't really "nothing" later on that afternoon when Jerry stopped by to collect my security badge and officially escort me out of the complex.

"Good luck in your new job," Jerry said as we headed up the main staircase to the promenade level.

"Thanks. And thank you for the going-away luncheon. Everybody seemed to have fun, and I appreciated the funny card and the generous gift certificate."

"Yeah. It's the least we could do."

"There was a pretty good mix of people there. I am grateful that everybody took time out of the office to be there, especially clients like Raul and Phillip."

"Phillip," Jerry said. "Did you invite him yourself?"

"No, why?" I asked.

Jerry stopped short as we emerged from the stairwell into the promenade level of the office complex. We stepped out of range of the stairwell doorway, just out of the main ebb and flow of pedestrian traffic. I saw that Jerry had that odd look on his face again. Pity.

"I am surprised that Phillip came at all. Look, since you are heading out, I've got to level with you. It was Phillip. He was in that management meeting. Phillip lobbied hard to have your position eliminated. At first, the others didn't go for it; you weren't on the list. They wanted to eliminate Evans. But Phillip persisted. He told them that the organization didn't need two lead computer performance analysts; that you weren't really all that good; and that he could do the job without you. He was pretty forceful, and they finally caved in."

I felt like I had been gut-punched, and everything suddenly became clear. About a month after I had come on board, Phillip and I had had a professional disagreement. I had been asked to create some graphs showing mainframe resource usage of the major groups of users, by week. My graphs had conflicted with the tabular reports that he had been producing, and upper management had pointed that out to him. Phillip had come to me to have me change my programs. But I had proven to him that my methodology was sound and showed him the flaw in his own logic. We had several uncomfortable sessions in which he had argued his point. However, I had backed up my arguments with references from the relevant literature, and he had finally capitulated. Phillip had ignored me for a few weeks thereafter. But he had eventually resumed our professional relationship and had come to me for advice every once in a while. So, I didn't think there was a problem between us. Wow. Talk about a lack of situational awareness!

Professional jealousy? Personal dislike? Holding a grudge? Who knew? And, at that point, who cared? I walked out of the building leaving that situation behind me and looking forward to the great new career possibilities that lay ahead of me.

**

Several years later, I was sitting at the desk in my home office getting ready to open an email containing the abstracts and first drafts of a bunch of technical papers that I had just received. I was one of the dozen Section Chairs for a very large software conference. As such, my main duty was to set up two days' worth of technical presentations in my particular subject-matter-specific section of the conference. A *Call for Papers* had gone out to thousands of the software's users a month or so beforehand. People from all over the country had submitted abstracts and rough drafts to the Conference Chair as per the instructions in the call for papers. He in turn had bundled them together by subject matter and sent them to the relevant Section Chairs. Some submissions went to the chair of the Statistics Section, some to the Data Visualization Section, and so forth for all of the sections that the conference comprised. Naturally, some submissions were forwarded to me so that I could evaluate their suitability for my own conference section.

I opened the email from the Conference Chair and downloaded the Zip file with the papers into the conference directory on my PC. I unzipped the Zip file, extracting fifteen papers into the directory. Then I returned to the email and read it. The very organized Conference Chair had included a table with the papers' titles, the submitters' names, and a box to check *Yes* or *No*—to indicate whether we were going to accept the paper or not.

Halfway down the table, my heart skipped a beat. There in black and white was Phillip's name. He had submitted an abstract and draft paper specifically to *my* section. I thought: *You've gotta be freaking kidding me!* My name was listed as the Section Chair in the Call for Papers. He had to have known that his paper would end up in my hands. I thought *how ironic—what goes around comes around!*—and rejected his paper outright. To hell with him!

I spent about ninety minutes reviewing the other papers in the batch and marked all of them for inclusion in the section I was building. There were some pretty cutting-edge papers in the batch! I updated the Yes/No column in the table and was getting ready to send the email back to the Conference Chair. But then I thought about Phillip's paper again and paused.

It was true that he had stabbed me in the back several years earlier. And it was true that I was in a position to be vindictive. But my parents saddled me with a burdensome sense of right and wrong, a sense that has plagued me all of my life. You know: "Do the right thing, Michael." "Work hard and you will get ahead, Michael." "Play by the rules and you will always come out on top, Michael." Yeah, crap like that. So, I held my breath, opened the Word document, and started to read Phillip's paper.

To say that it was god-awful would have been an understatement. It wasn't really a technical paper; it was the crime scene of an English grammar and diction mass murder. Every writing rule in the book had been broken. Run on sentences? Check. First-person narrative? Check. Hackneyed clichés? Check. Misspellings? Check. Code examples and graphs without labels or explanations? Check. Missing references section? Check. Self-congratulatory expositions on how he had cleverly resolved coding issues? Check. Well-worn topic and obvious solutions to the programming problem presented? Check.

Fortunately, he had not only mutilated the rules of English grammar and the rules of business writing, but he had also not followed the guidelines for the paper layout. So, I did reject the paper. It was one of the easiest rejections that I had ever done. Fourteen papers accepted; one rejected . . . with extreme prejudice.

A couple of weeks later, I received an email from the Conference Chair. He told me that he had received several frantic emails from Phillip after sending out the rejection notices. Phillip had contested the rejection of his paper, claiming that it was technically sound and cutting edge. He wrote that the Section Chair—me—obviously didn't understand the subject material if he was rejecting the paper. He further told the Conference Chair that if his paper was not accepted, his management would not let him attend the conference.

Now, that made me smile! I sent a message back to the Conference Chair telling him the paper was a piece of crap and would absolutely not go into my section. I reminded him that he chose me as the Section Chair because of my technical expertise and should respect my professional judgment. *All right, all right!* he responded. *Just double-checking. Relax. I always back up my section chairs.*

Later that year, I did not see Phillip at the conference. But, then again, I wasn't really looking for him in the crowd of over 3,500 attendees. I had a lot of duties to perform as a Section Chair. I concentrated on running my section, attending technical presentations of interest to me, and networking with my peers. Overall, it was a great conference.

***

Of course, it was fated to happen. At the next year's conference, I was just parting ways with a colleague as we walked out of the demo room when I came face to face with Phillip, who was heading in. He stopped short about three paces in front of me. Phillip gave me a glare that said: *You rejected my paper and screwed me out of going to last year's conference, and I hate you.* Not intimidated, I glared back: *You put my livelihood and career in jeopardy, and I hate you.* After about 20 seconds of staring each other down, Phillip pointedly sneered, walked around me, and disappeared into the demo room.

We passed each other several more times during the conference. Each time that we did, we locked eyes and stared each other down as we passed. Neither of us was willing to let it go, neither of us was willing to look away, neither of us was willing to give in, neither of us was willing to be an adult.

On the last day of the conference, I was in the back of the ballroom, where the closing session was just wrapping up. I saw Phillip getting up from a chair to head out with the rest of the departing crowd. Since I was standing by the doors, he would have to pass right by me. Should I turn and walk away or stare him down again? Unfortunately, I heard my parent's voices in my head: "Do the right thing, Michael." "Work hard and you will get ahead, Michael." "Play by the rules and you will always come out on top, Michael." And I softened.

I stepped forward as Phillip approached the door and smiled.

Phillip stopped suddenly when he saw me. He looked panicked like he thought that I was going to assault him.

"Hey," I said. "Look, we are going to be seeing each other every year at this conference. What are we going to do, just continue to glare at one another? I'm not really mad at you, and I don't want any hostilities."

"Listen man, I wasn't the one who tried to get you laid off of that contract," he lied with a straight face.

"I know. And the Conference Chair told us we had to reject all papers that didn't strictly follow the guidelines," I lied back to him with a straight face. I extended my hand. "No hard feelings?"

He took my hand and shook it.

"No. We're good," he said with a broad smile.

"Great," I said. "Have a safe journey home. See you next year."

As time and circumstances would have it, I never saw Phillip again. Not ever. But I did hear from him. Once.

A couple of years later, I decided to submit one of my technical papers to a national conference whose focus was computer performance evaluation and capacity planning. Since the main topic of my paper was boosting software performance, I felt that it was a good crossover paper and very likely to be accepted. Several weeks after my submission to the Conference Chair, I received a reply. But it was not from the Conference Chair. It was from the guy who was obviously the Section Chair for the track that my paper would have been in. It simply read:

Michael,

R-E-J-E-C-T-E-D!!!!!!!!!!!!!!!!!!!!!!!!!!!!!!!!!!!!!!!

—Phillip

1011 GOING OFF SCRIPT

They say that knowledge is power. They also say that knowledge in the wrong hands is not a good thing. Thinking back on it, I guess that Bob and I had the *wrong hands*.

Bob and I were working in a large federal data center nestled in an office park in the Washington, DC, suburbs. We were part of a seven-person team whose job was to monitor the performance and capacity of the large mainframe computers housed in the data center. Both of us had a lot of systems programming experience and were pretty well versed in mainframe internals. So, it was not surprising that Bob found it.

"Hey, come on over and take look at this," Bob called across the narrow passageway that separated our cubicles.

"What have you got there?" I asked sauntering over to Bob's cubicle.

"I found the login scripts that our group invokes when they log into the mainframe," he said, proudly. "Check them out."

The login scripts contained the instructions used to interact between the programmer and the mainframe when you first started an interactive session. It queried the programmer for a user ID and then communicated it to the mainframe. If the user ID was valid, the login script next asked for the programmer's password. Once that was conveyed and verified, the login script completed the login by specifying the proper user account and establishing an interactive session on the mainframe. At that point, the programmer could write programs, access files, and do all of the types of things that one did on a mainframe computer.

"I'm surprised that each one of us has an individual login script," Bob said. "I would have thought there would be only one for the entire group."

"I'll bet it is set up that way in case they need to be customized," I replied.

"Customized?"

"Yeah. Suppose you needed to log into a different unit's mainframe account. Or suppose you needed to get special messages while logging in," I explained.

"Like what kind of special messages?" Bob asked.

"I don't know. Like . . . um . . ." And then I got a nasty idea. "Hey," I said, "I've got a nasty idea!"

"Oh, no!" said Bob. He had heard my nasty ideas a few other times and knew we were in for some fun.

"What if we modified the login scripts a bit so that they sent some *very special* messages to some of our group members? Nothing too bad, just something fun," I offered.

"Right," said Bob. He paused a moment to think. "Sharon and Roger are the best candidates. They are the least computer savvy people in our group, and hence the most vulnerable."

Sharon was a rising computer programmer assigned to our unit. She had an extensive background in Microsoft Office products and was just coming up to speed on mainframe computer programming languages. Roger was the manager of our unit. He was a grizzled veteran of twenty-odd years of government service, all in the computer programming sector. He had a working knowledge of computer performance and capacity planning, but was more managerial than technical. It was late in the day, and both Sharon and Roger were long gone. So the coast was clear.

"Great," I said, "Let's do this!"

I went back to my cubicle and wheeled my chair across the aisle to Bob's office space. By the time I got back, he had already made backup copies of Sharon's and Roger's original login scripts. That way, we could restore them after our little joke.

Bob hunched over his keyboard and began typing in earnest. I leaned over his shoulder and watched. We traded ideas back and forth, and he programmed them into the login scripts. Whenever we thought one of the modified login scripts was ready, we would execute it to verify that it was displaying the *right* messages. We laughed like idiots every time we went through one. After about an hour, we were satisfied with our results. We headed out the door, agreeing to make sure that we both got in bright and early the next day to watch the results of our hard work.

In the morning, we both said "good morning" to Sharon as she breezed past us to her own cubicle carrying her usual 20-ounce coffee and breakfast pastry. Something in Bob's voice made her stop, turn around, and go back to his doorway.

"What?" she asked suspiciously.

"Nothing!" Bob exclaimed innocently.

"Oh, okay," said Sharon, "It's just that you sound a bit odd this morning . . ."

"He sounds odd every morning," I ventured from my own cubicle.

Sharon laughed and then continued onward. We heard her put her things away. We heard her make her usual call to her husband to tell him she was at the office and discuss what they would be eating that night. We heard her open the wrapper to her pastry and pour her paper cup of coffee into the mug she kept at her desk. Then, finally, we heard it; Sharon switched on her desktop computer to log into the mainframe.

When she entered her user ID Sharon got this series of messages, each appearing after a ten-second interval:

```
IKJ00666 MVS/ESA LOGON FOR USER: Sharon NOT IN
PROGRESS

00666IKJ MVS/ESA VALIDITY CHECK FOR ATTACHED KEYBOARD

00666IKJ MVS/ESA KEYBOARD IS BELOW OPERATIONAL
TEMPERATURE

00IKJ666 MVS/ESA PLEASE WARM KEYBOARD BEFORE
PROCEEDING

IOK6J066 MVS/ESA WARM KEYBOARD BY PRE-TYPING EACH KEY
```

"What?" Sharon exclaimed loudly. "What is this? I've never seen this before! It's telling me that my keyboard needs to be warmed up."

"Um, they did a systems upgrade last night," Bob called over the cubicle wall. "The new software is supposed to be more sensitive than the old version. I would just do whatever it tells you to do."

"But it doesn't make sense," said Sharon. "It just doesn't make sense . . ."

Then, we were rewarded by the sound of her typing—and typing fast. She was *pre-typing* every key to warm up the keyboard as instructed. Bob and I were convulsing so hard with silent laughter that we nearly fell out of our chairs.

"Done," Sharon finally said triumphantly. "Hmm . . . it's still hanging." Then, suddenly, "Now what?"

Her monitor had refreshed and a new series of messages began scrolling down:

```
IKJ00666 MVS/ESA LOGON FOR USER: Sharon NOT IN
PROGRESS

00666IKJ MVS/ESA VALIDITY CHECK FOR ATTACHED PRINTER

666IKJ00 MVS/ESA PAPER IN PRINTER MOUNTED
INCORRECTLY

00IKJ666 MVS/ESA USE OFF-WHITE PAPER ONLY IN PRINTER

IOK6J066 MVS/ESA IT READS BETTER AND AVOIDS MVS
ERRORS
```

Sharon read each statement aloud as it flowed across her screen. Bob and I were heaving with laughter.

"That just doesn't make any sense!" Sharon exclaimed. "How would it know what type of paper is in the printer?"

That's when Bob really lost it. He guffawed out loud and then started laughing and laughing and laughing. That triggered my own outburst. I laughed so hard that tears were streaming down my cheeks.

Sharon burst out of her office and into our doorways.

"You guys!" she exclaimed with a big smile on her face. She slugged Bob in the arm, and threw a pen at me.

"You had me going there for a minute, there. That was great!"

When we got back our composure, we told her about Roger's revised logon script. Her smile became as devilish as our own as she joined the conspiracy. Because it was about time for Roger to come into the office, she hung out at our cubicles to wait for the big show.

Roger arrived some minutes later. His manager's cubicle was, understandably, bigger than our worker-bee cubicles and located just across the main thoroughfare that ran through the cubicle farm. Roger took his coat off and hung it on the rack. He took some papers out of the inter-office mailbox that hung outside his cubicle and put them on his desk. He sorted through the papers for a few minutes. Then he made a quick telephone call to somebody. Roger didn't notice that he was under surveillance, because whenever he looked up, our six eyes would quickly flick away from him and back to a big printout that we were supposedly discussing in the aisle between our cubicles.

Finally, Roger switched on his computer. When he entered his user ID, Roger got this series of messages, each appearing after a ten-second interval:

```
IKJOO666 MVS/ESA *** A T T E N T I O N ****

OO666IKJ MVS/ESA A RECORD OF THIS INCIDENT HAS BEEN
RECORDED

OO666IKJ MVS/ESA ALL FILES IN YOUR GROUP'S PRODUCTION
PROGRAMMING LIBRARY

OO666IKJ MVS/ESA HAVE BEEN DELETED AS REQUESTED

OOIKJ666 MVS/ESA PRESS <ENTER> TO CONTINUE DELETING
PRODUCTION DATA SETS
```

"What?" Roger exclaimed, "I didn't do anything! I *didn't . . . do . . . any . . . thing*! No!"

He jumped up from his keyboard as if it had attacked him and looked over at us for help. But he did not see three systems programmers ready, willing, and able to jump in and help him in

88

his time of need. Instead, what he saw was three systems programmers doubled-over and laughing so hard that they were crying. Moments later, when the shock was gone and the recognition had set in, he was laughing, too.

1100 THE COFFEE MAKER(S)

We were two hotshot application programmers eager to make a big impact on our organization, a federal agency located in downtown Washington, DC. Most of the agency's programming staff had been assigned to a mega project that was working on transitioning the organization's computing platform from central mainframes to distributed UNIX servers. Tom and I had been given the mandate to fill in the gaps in service by helping anybody who had a need for one-shot programming assignments. We could be tapped to create ad hoc reports, quick data analysis, database extract files, graphs and charts, data validation and acceptance testing, and a host of other tasks for anyone who needed to have them done. In essence, we were a *guerilla programming group* that could strike wherever we could do the most good without getting bogged down on a particular project.

The Monday that we moved from the data center to our new office in the historic headquarters building in Washington, DC, marked the official beginning of our new assignment. The move took all day to complete. The morning was spent unloading the boxes of books, files, and office supplies that the movers had brought from our offices at the data center over the weekend. The afternoon was spent working with the systems staff to get our workstations configured correctly so that we could access the mainframe systems. At the end of that day, our office was set up, and we were ready for business.

One entered our office through an oversized wooden door that had a large opaque glass window set into the top half of it with the room number stenciled in black on the frosted glass. The first thing visitors saw when they came into our office was our two big, clunky, metal desks facing the doorway, with a slim aisle between them. In front of each desk was a waist-high, metal filing cabinet with drawers facing towards the center of the room. Behind the desks was a window that looked out onto 14th Street. The room had a high ceiling and was well lit by hanging light fixtures. Like most offices in historic federal office buildings, ours was a bit worn out from the many, many, many previous occupants. But that did not matter to us. We thought that our new office was an amazing base from which to launch our programming forays.

That Thursday morning, I waved at Tom.

"Hey, I'm going to make a coffee run. Want any?" I asked.

Every programmer knows that coffee is the oil that fuels programmatic creativity. There is something locked deep inside of those *Canephora* or *Arabica* beans that are grown in Brazil, or Vietnam, or Indonesia, or Columbia, or Ethiopia, or a host of other coffee-belt countries that enhances clarity and performance. *Programming* performance, that is!

"Yeah," Tom said, pausing his iPod and taking out his earbuds. "I could use a *large*. Make sure to bring back some sugars this time."

Then, because he was always thinking, he came up with the bright idea.

"You know what we could really use in here?" he asked. "Our own coffee maker. Then we wouldn't have to always be running out for coffee."

It was a great idea. Our building did not have a cafeteria in it so we had to stop for coffee someplace between the Metro and our office on the way in. The nearest coffee shop was actually one long block away. So, every time we wanted a cup, we would have to leave the office, trudge down Constitution Avenue, and head down 12th Street to the Old Post Office Pavilion. Not a great hardship, but not exactly convenient.

"Brilliant idea!" I commented. "Hmmm . . . I'll tell you what: I have a 20-percent-off coupon, so I'll pick up a coffee maker on Saturday. How about if you get us some nice coffees and coffee making supplies?"

"Can do," said Tom. "I hope that you like the strong stuff because I tend to like dark roasts."

"Yep, sounds good to me." The agreement made, Tom went back to work and I went out the door.

Tom was already in the office when I showed up on Monday morning carrying an oversized white shopping bag containing a 10-cup coffee maker and a box of coffee filters.

"Check this out," Tom said with a grand sweep of his left hand towards the filing cabinet in front of his desk.

The filing cabinet had a mini, red-and-white checkered tablecloth spread out across the top. On it were two wooden bowls; one containing non-dairy creamers, the other containing packets of sugar and sugar substitutes. Beside the bowls there was a Styrofoam cup full of multicolored plastic coffee stirrers. Most importantly, there were three bags of already-ground, gourmet dark roast coffee: Italian, Sumatra, and French.

"Nice!" I said. "You did well. And so did I. The coffee maker was marked down, *and* I got the 20 percent discount, too. Also, it has a special feature built into the bottom outtake spout. That feature stops the coffee from flowing into the pot when the pot is moved away from the coffee maker. So we can pour coffee anytime—even when coffee is still brewing. Pretty cool, eh?"

I put the bag down on my desk, opened the top, and lifted the box out of it. The bag fell to the floor. Tom swept it aside with a swing of his leg. I held the box up for Tom to see the picture on the side.

Tom whistled. "Wow. She's a thing of beauty!" he said.

Tom walked around his desk and opened the top drawer. He took out a pair of scissors and walked back to where I was standing.

"Here," he said handing me the scissors.

I rested the box on the front of my desk and cut the strip of clear tape that held the top of the box in place. I opened the top and saw that the entire contents were held between two big square pieces of Styrofoam packing. I took the top of the

Styrofoam in both hands and shook it free from the box. The box fell to the floor. Tom swept it aside with a swing of his leg.

I cut the tape that held the two halves of the Styrofoam packing together and separated the coffee maker unit from the Styrofoam packing material. The Styrofoam fell to the floor. Tom swept it aside with a swing of his leg.

The ten-cup, clear glass pot was sitting in its place on the heating element of the coffee maker. The pot was long and cylindrical with a slightly curved bottom. It had a black plastic spout around the top and a black plastic band stretching around the circumference of the pot about two inches from the bottom. A bold black plastic handle ran along one side affixed at the top to the back of the spout area and to the black ring towards the bottom. There were white lines and markings along one side: 2 Cups, 4 Cups, 6 Cups, 8 Cups, 10 Cups. The lid had a hinge at the top of the handle, so you could swing it upward with a press of your thumb. The lid had at its center a dome about two inches in diameter with a hole in the center, through which the coffee would drip when it was being brewed. The instruction brochure, warranty, and some advertising material were stuffed inside the coffee pot.

I placed the coffee maker on the filing cabinet in front of my desk and plugged it into a wall outlet. Then I removed the pot. I popped the lid up with my thumb and dumped the instructions, warranty, and other papers onto the top of my desk.

"Give that to me," Tom said, pointing to the coffee pot. "I'll go to the men's room, wash it out, and fill it with water."

I handed the pot to Tom, and he went out the door. The men's room was inconveniently located on the opposite side of the building from us. We had to walk out into the hall, turn left and walk about thirty feet, turn right and go down the long hallway, turn right at the end of the long hallway, and there it was halfway down the other short hall on the right-hand side. It was about a three-minute walk. So, I had a few minutes to make preparations.

When Tom left, I went back to the shopping bag that was on the floor and picked it up. I fished inside the bag and took out the box of coffee filters. I opened the box, separated one filter from the others, and set it down. Then I placed the box of filters on Tom's filing cabinet beside the cup of coffee stirrers.

I took the scissors from Tom's desk and cut across the top of one of the bags of coffee labeled *Sumatra Dark Roast*. It was already ground, so I poured a heaping portion of it into the coffee filter. The coffee maker's swing-out filter basket was on a hinge right above where the coffee pot would sit. I swung the filter basket out and placed the filter full of Sumatra dark roast into it. Then I swung the filter basket back into place.

Tom arrived with the pot full of water. He brushed past me, opened the lid on the top of the coffee maker, and poured the water into the unit's reservoir. I closed the lid. Tom placed the pot onto the warming plate and hit the *ON* switch. We both stepped back and waited with our eyes glued to the coffee maker.

The coffee maker came to life with a gurgle and a hiss. The warming plate beneath the pot began to glow, coloring the bottom of the pot a light pink. Unseen within the coffee maker, a resistive heating element heated an aluminum tube that ran from the reservoir to the showerhead in the top of the coffee maker above the filter basket. As the water heated, bubbles formed and forced

95

water upward into the showerhead. The water dripped evenly from the showerhead into the coffee grounds within the filter basket. The hot water flowed through the coffee grounds causing a hydrolytic reaction to take place. Water-soluble alkaloids (caffeine and trigonelline), carbohydrates, and proteins were liberated from the coffee grounds and dissolved into the hot water, giving birth to liquid coffee.

Moments later, the first precious drops of dark brown fluid began dripping from the bottom of the outtake spout, through the hole in the domed lid of the pot, and down into the bottom of the pot. It was tentative and slow at first, but then a steady stream began to flow in a semi-straight brown line down into the center of the pot. The wonderful smell of fresh-brewed coffee filled our office as the liquid steadily filled the pot. We stood mesmerized, watching the fruit of our labor. The brown liquid hit the 2-Cup line, then the 4-Cup line, then the 6-Cup line, then the 8-Cup line, and continued towards the 10-Cup goal. Finally, a series of hissing and deep gurgling sounds signaled the end of the water's trip up from the water well through the filter and into the pot.

"Check this out," said Tom, proudly. He reached into a plastic bag that had been sitting on the front of his desk and produced two thick, blue coffee mugs. Tom held them up for inspection, and I could see that they had the agency logo stenciled on one side.

"Awesome!" I said taking one.

We poured two cups of coffee. Tom stirred two creamers and two sugars into his. I stirred half of one creamer into mine. Then we smiled at our handiwork, clinked our cups together in a salute, and had that first taste of coffee making success. And it was good. It was very, very good.

Business was good, too. It was very, very good. Word had spread about our internal consulting services, and we had a steady stream of people coming in to request various data extracts, one-shot analyses, graphs, charts, and tables. Our visitors often noted the large coffee pot with its ample supply of extra coffee. Since it was the only source of fresh coffee on our floor of the building, some of them brought empty coffee cups on their return trips. Sometimes, our colleagues would drop by without needing any programming work just to talk over a cup of coffee. So, during those first few weeks, the office was full of good programming, good smells, good conversation, and good vibes. Life was good. It was very, very good. But, of course, nothing lasts forever.

One day, I was torn from my programming reverie by a sputtering, hissing sound coming from the coffee maker. I looked over the right side of my monitor at the coffee maker, but didn't see what was wrong at first. I glanced over at Tom.

Somehow, he had heard it, too. He paused his iPod, pulled out his earbuds, pushed his chair back, and squeezed between our desks. He got to the coffee maker as I was rising out of my chair.

"What the hell?" Tom exclaimed.

I joined him and saw the problem. Coffee had backed up in the filter basket and had been flowing over the top. There was a big puddle of golden brown liquid on the top of the filing cabinet. A small waterfall of French dark roast was cascading down the far side of the filing cabinet into a little pond of coffee on the floor between the filing cabinet and the door. The sputtering was coming from the coffee that had dribbled onto the warming plate.

Tom snapped the coffee maker's power switch *OFF* with a quick swipe of his hand.

"What happened?" I asked rhetorically.

Tom pulled the quarter-filled pot from the warming plate and set it aside. He carefully swung the filter basket out and we looked at the mess of water and grounds that filled it to the brim. Then we looked at the mechanism beneath the filter basket. It was the special feature that was supposed to snap closed to prevent coffee from dripping out when the pot was removed. The mechanism was a short piece of black plastic on a spring connected to the bottom of the filter basket. When the pot was in place, pressure against the spring kept it away from the opening in the bottom of the filter basket, letting coffee drip. When the pot was removed, the spring snapped the piece of plastic shut so that it plugged the opening in the bottom of the filter basket.

"Looks like the plastic arm got stuck shut somehow," Tom said. "It plugged the opening and the coffee backed up and spilled over the top."

"That shouldn't happen." I said. "I don't see how it possibly can."

"Me neither, but we can worry about that later," said Tom, unplugging the unit. "Get some paper towels so that we can get this mess cleaned up."

I opened the door, went out into the hallway, and walked to the men's room on the far side of the building. From the dispenser, I pulled out one paper towel after another until I had a big handful. Then I returned to the office.

"Hold this and help me," Tom said. He leaned down, picked up my round metal trashcan, and handed it to me. I grabbed it with both hands and held it close by.

Tom took hold of the coffee maker and started tilting it while steadying the overflowing coffee basket. I moved the trashcan under the basket and a goodly portion of the mixture of grounds and water flowed over the side and into the white plastic trash bag inside the trashcan. Because there was still water in the coffee maker's reservoir, we couldn't completely invert the unit and empty all of the mess that was in the brewing basket. Nonetheless, we managed to pour a lot of the mess out into the trashcan.

"Okay, that's enough," said Tom. "I'll get this down to the men's room and get it cleaned up."

I opened the door for Tom, and he walked slowly down the hallway holding the coffee maker delicately with two hands.

I took a wad of paper towels and started sopping up the mess on the top of the filing cabinet. It took two hands full of paper towels to get the liquid absorbed and a third clump to get the surface dry. Then I sopped up the puddle on the floor. I had to move the filing cabinet back a few inches to get the coffee that had seeped under it. I completed the cleanup by wiping the brown stain that ran down the far side of the filing cabinet.

Tom returned looking pretty aggravated. He placed the cleaned-up coffee maker back in its accustomed spot. We examined the plastic arm on the bottom of the filter basket. We manually popped it open and closed, open and closed, open and closed. Then, we pushed the coffee pot under it and pulled it out; under and out; under and out. The plastic arm worked perfectly.

"What do you think?" Tom asked.

"Well, only one way to find out," I replied. "Empty the pot and get some more water. I'll get the coffee ready."

Tom headed back to the men's room with the coffee pot. I opened the Ethiopian dark roast, measured a heaping portion into a new filter, and then put the filter into the filter basket and swung it shut. When Tom returned, he poured the water into the coffee maker's reservoir, closed the lid, and placed the pot on top of the heating element. I hit the *ON* switch. We both stepped back and waited with our eyes glued to the coffee maker.

The coffee maker came to life with its customary gurgle and hiss. The warming plate beneath the pot glowed a light pink. A minute later, the first drops of dark brown fluid began dripping from the bottom of the outtake spout, through the hole in the lid, and down into the bottom of the pot. We watched as the pot slowly filled with coffee, both of us apprehensive that, at any moment, it would once again back up and overflow. Finally, the hissing, deep gurgling sound signaled the end of the process. 10 cups—the pot was full. Success!

"Okay, then . . ." Tom smiled. "Coffee?"

"Yeah," I said. "Coffee!"

We poured two cups of coffee. Tom stirred two creamers and two sugars into his. I stirred half of one creamer into mine. We took exploratory sips and then smiled at our success.

"I'm glad that's over," said Tom.

"Yeah," I said before taking a long, slow, satisfying pull of my coffee. "Me, too!"

But it was not over; not by a long shot. The problem occurred again on Friday. The following week, we had two overflows. After that, the coffee maker would overflow on random days. There was never a pattern; never a precursor event; never an indication that we would have an overspill on a particular day. It just happened. Sometimes we had coffee; sometimes we had a mess. Sometimes we would try a second time; sometimes we were just too demoralized, and one of us would go out to buy coffee.

Coffee making became a major event in our office during which all programming work would cease. Tom and I would first make sure that we had plenty of paper towels on hand and that my trash can was close to the filing cabinet. Then we would get the coffee maker ready for action. Next, we would toggle the plastic arm open and closed, open and closed, open and closed to confirm that it was not stuck. We would pull the pot in and out, in and out, in and out to verify that the plastic arm was working correctly with the top of the coffee pot lid. Finally, we would turn the switch to the ON position and wait. Neither of us could work after the switch was pushed. We both stared intently at the filter basket, ready to spring into action should we see even the slightest drop of coffee overflow it. We both strained our ears, keenly listening to every sound that came from the coffee maker, ready to turn it off should we hear the sputtering of coffee dripping onto the warming plate.

Sadly, we became very good at cleaning up the mess. We kept a large stack of paper towels on Tom's filing cabinet next to the Styrofoam cup of coffee stirrers. We had purchased a box of white plastic trash bags and now kept my trashcan adjacent to the filing cabinet at all times. We had assigned jobs when an overspill occurred. I would turn the unit off and unplug it. Tom would pick it up, and swing the filter basket out. I would pick up the trashcan and hold it under the coffee maker. Tom would dump as much as he could out into the trashcan. Then Tom would set the unit down, grab the edges of the soggy filter and gingerly lift the filter—water, grounds, and all—out, and drop it into the trashcan. I would sop up the remaining coffee in the filter basket with paper towels while Tom cleaned any spillover that had puddled on my filing cabinet. We could complete the entire cleanup process in about five minutes.

When we finally hit three overspill events in a row one week, we just gave up. There was no discussion or formal admission of defeat as we cleaned up that final mess. Just a silent understanding between the two of us that we were done. The next day, I bought a large cup of coffee from a kiosk at the Old Post Office Pavilion on my way into work. When I entered the office, I saw that Tom had a 20-ounce paper coffee cup sitting on his desk next to a half-eaten donut. The coffee maker wasn't even plugged in.

As time went by, the front half of our office assumed an air of decrepitude much like that of an abandoned farmstead or a long-vacant building lot. On Tom's filing cabinet, a full bag of French roast and a half-bag of Italian dark roast sat upright, unused and forgotten. The non-dairy creamers and packets of sugar and sugar substitutes sat neglected in their bowls. The Styrofoam cup lay on its side with the multi-colored coffee stirrers spilled out across the checkered tablecloth. The box of coffee filters and the pile of paper towels sat derelict and forsaken. On my filing cabinet, the coffee maker stood unplugged, silent, empty, and abandoned. A thin film of dust layered the top of the coffee maker and the exposed filing cabinet on either side of it.

It wasn't until it was dark and cold that I realized how much life and light and joy and wonder the coffee maker had brought to our office. It had been the focal point of the room, much the same way fire pits had been the focal point of primeval man's campsites. We had tended to and fussed over the coffee maker the same way that ancient people had tended to and fussed over their fires. The first person into the office in the morning made the first brew of the day. We watched the level of coffee in the pot as the morning progressed and made a second—and sometimes a third—pot when we had a lot of coffee-drinking guests drop by. Around one-thirty or two o'clock we would make an after-lunch pot and keep it handy until quitting time. Between coffee-making rounds, either or both of us would clean the pot, filter basket, and any mess on either of the filing cabinets. We watched the levels of non-dairy creamer and sugars carefully, and replaced them as necessary. These small chores were fun and provided a nice diversion from our programming tasks.

The death of the coffee maker cast a cloud over the work environment. Our once-happy office became just like any other business-only office on that floor of the building. Our programming work seemed to get harder, we had fewer drop-in visitors, and the office itself looked shabbier than we could remember. Tom stayed plugged into his iPod for longer periods of time and didn't make much small talk. I started going out for lunch instead of eating at my desk as I had done beforehand. Though we continued to do solid programming work that made a difference to the organization, the office had taken on an aura of gloom and the dreary feeling of unrealized ambitions.

"Hey, I'm going to make a coffee run, want any?" I asked one day as I put on my coat.

"Yeah," Tom said, pausing his iPod and taking out his earbuds. "Make it a large and be sure to bring back some sugars."

Then, because he was always thinking, he came up with another bright idea.

"Wait a minute," he said excitedly. "Wait . . . just . . . one . . . minute!"

Tom pushed back his chair, squeezed between the desks, and went over to the coffee maker. He slid the pot out from between the warming plate and the filter basket and handed it to me. He swung the filter basket open and dropped to his knees, staring at the bedeviling plastic arm on its bottom. Tom grabbed the plastic arm with his right hand and pulled it down as far as it would go. Then he braced the side of the filter basket with his left hand and yanked his right hand down fast and hard. With a loud snap, the plastic arm sheared off, leaving an unobstructed hole in the bottom of the filter basket.

Tom ceremoniously threw the plastic arm into the trashcan with a neat overhand shot.

"Well," he said. "That's that! How about we brew ourselves a fresh pot of dark roast?"

"Are you kidding me?" I yelled. "Are you freaking kidding me? All of the time we spent cleaning up those messes, all of that frustration, all of that anger, all of that anxiety—and the fix was *that* simple!"

"Don't sweat it," said Tom opening the bag of Italian dark roast with a sly smile. "We are *software* guys. That was a *hardware* problem."

1101 THE SWORD OF DAMOCLES

This whole incident began because of my lack of spatial acuity. Or maybe it was my lack of architectural imagination. Regardless—what might have been perceived as a weakness ended up providing a positive outcome.

We were working in a large federal data center nestled in an office park in the Washington, DC, suburbs. The data center was a vast, two-story building surrounded by a parking lot. The entire complex was ringed by an eight-foot-high barbed wire fence and only accessible through a guard gate that was manned 24/7. Because it was such a hassle to check in and out at the guard gate, we would more often than not eat lunch in the break room and then walk all the way around the parking lot to get some exercise. It was on one of those walks that we got into a discussion about the building's interior architecture.

The "we" in this narrative were my fellow computer performance analyst colleague Bob and I. We both worked for a consulting firm that had a contract for monitoring the performance and capacity of the large mainframe computers housed in the data center. Bob and I were part of a seven-person performance and capacity planning unit. Our unit had recently been moved to new cubicle office space deep within the data center. The new office space was in a *raised floor* area of the building that was recently reclaimed from part of the computer room. It had a raised white floor, small one-person cubicles, and a suspended ceiling. Because it was still on the same climate-control system as the computer room, the office area was always cold. Cold in the winter. Cold in the summer. Cold!

"Hey, Bob," I said as we strolled around the data center one day, "that's about where our offices are located. Somewhere behind that wall."

"Right," said Bob.

"But that doesn't make any sense," I said. "If you look at the building, you can see that there are offices on the second floor above our office space," I explained.

"Right," said Bob.

"We have a raised floor and a suspended ceiling . . ." I offered, hoping that he would see my point.

"Right," said Bob.

"So, there is likely two feet of space beneath the raised floor. Then the office stretches about ten feet up to the drop ceiling. And then there has to be at least two or three feet beyond the drop ceiling to the real ceiling," I pressed on. I paused expectantly.

"Right," said Bob.

"Don't you see the problem with the dimensions?" I asked.

"Nope," said Bob.

"Well, if you add two feet plus ten feet plus another three feet, you get fifteen feet. Look," I said with a sweep of my hand, "That second story is less than fifteen feet from the first story. There is no way that our area can physically exist in there."

"Oh, right!" said Bob.

"Hmmm . . . ," I mused, pressing onward. "Our offices are towards the interior of the building. I wonder if the upper floor offices just do not penetrate that deeply into the building. C'mon, let's find out!"

"Right," said Bob.

We went back into the building, took the center staircase just off the lobby, and went up to the second floor. We paced down the hallways that were along the same side of the building as our own office space. Bob and I tried to determine just how deep those hallways extended from the front of the building towards the middle and back of the structure. They seemed to go about halfway to the center of the building, which would put that part of the second story directly over where our office space was located. It didn't make sense.

"Only one thing to do," I told Bob. "We are going to have to go downstairs and look above the raised ceiling. That should tell us how much clearance there is."

"Right," said Bob.

We pounded down the back staircase, turned right at the

bottom, went down the small hallway, and then opened the door to our office area. A blast of refrigerated air hit our faces as we went through and walked over to our cubicles.

"First things first," I said to Bob. I went over to the utility room and got a suction-cup tile lifter. I took it to the middle of the aisle that ran between Bob's cubicle and my own. I stuck the tile lifter to the center floor tile panel, lifted it up, and set it aside. A wave of cool air wafted out of the two-by-two foot open space. A score of color-coded cables of various thicknesses snaked through the space underneath the square hole in the raised floor.

"Can you give me something to measure this with," I asked Bob.

"Right." Bob handed me the stainless steel computer ruler he kept on his desk.

I leaned down into the hole, inserted the ruler between the cables, and measured the gap from the cement floor to the top of the raised floor.

"Yup, that's two feet all right."

I set the ruler aside and then replaced the floor tile, making sure that it was securely fitted into its slot. When I got up I could see that Bob was raising the seat of his office chair to its highest setting. When he was finished with that, he wheeled the chair to the middle of his cubicle.

By now, we had an audience. The other members of the team had heard us removing the floor tile and were curious about what we were going to do with the suspended ceiling.

"Steady me," Bob said as he took hold of both arms of his

swivel chair and unsteadily mounted it.

I steadied him by putting my hands on his hips at the beltline on each side. Once he felt secure, Bob let go of the chair's arms and slowly raised himself up. He stopped when he was at full height and took stock of his balance. Then he slowly raised his arms towards the tile in the raised ceiling that hung over his desk. His fingertips could just barely reach it.

"Steady me," Bob said again and raised himself up on his tiptoes on the chair.

He was then able to push against the ceiling tile with his fingertips. At first it didn't budge, having apparently settled solidly into place long ago. But, as Bob grunted and strained, a fine smattering of dust and ceiling tile debris began to drift downward from one of the edges. Then one end of the ceiling tile popped completely free up into the raised ceiling space. Bob had not been expecting that and was still applying full pressure. The top end of the ceiling tile popped up to about a 35-degree angle, releasing the hold of the lower edge of the tile from its bracket.

"Look out!" Bob yelled as the ceiling tile slipped past his fingers and crashed onto his desk.

"Oh, wow!" I exclaimed as the shock of the sudden noise subsided.

Then I started laughing. Everybody started laughing. Everybody, that is, except Bob. He stood on the chair with his face peering intently into the dimly lit space above. His face was ashen, and I thought that I felt him trembling.

"No way," he said. "No way! Get me down. *I want to get down!*"

I helped him get down from the chair, and he pushed past me out of his cubicle.

"Look at that," Bob demanded, gesturing to the gaping hole in the ceiling. "It's been there all of this time. I could have been killed at any moment. There is no way that I am going to sit there anymore!"

I got up on the wobbly chair and looked up into the gap. It took my eyes a moment to adjust to the semi-darkness. But then I saw what Bob was talking about. The actual ceiling looked to be about six feet above the suspended ceiling. There, above where Bob normally sat, hung a thick, threaded, three-foot-long metal tie rod. The heavy metal tie rod was suspended by a thin electrical wire that was fastened to an eyelet at the top of the rod and an eyelet in the cement ceiling. If the electrical wire had broken, the tie rod would have plummeted directly down to where Bob normally sat analyzing the performance and capacity of the data center's mainframe computers.

We reported the problem to the building maintenance crew. They removed the tie rod that night and stated that the wire had been strong and that Bob had never really been in any danger. But they could not explain why it was there in the first place. And their safety explanation did not placate Bob. He insisted on switching to a different cubicle. But before he took up residence in the new one, he had me help him lift the ceiling tile above it so that he could have a good, long, thorough look-see into the space above his head.

1110 PRACTICAL MATH

The *Twist* data center craze began one bright Tuesday in May at the end of Techie Lunch Hour. Later on, many people would claim that I was the one who had started the whole thing. But it wasn't really me. It is true that I had a role in its beginning, but I always felt more like a victim of circumstance than a trendsetter.

Techie Lunch Hour was the unofficial name we had given to the one-to-two o'clock time slot when the hardcore computer nerds, geeks, and hackers took over the data center's large break room. Techie Lunch Hour was a kind of second seating for the not-so-cool kids: the mainframe system programmers, the UNIX administrators, the Java programmers, the computer performance analysts, the web programmers, and the database administrators. It was a time when we could be among our own kind to relax and talk about bits and bytes, memory registers, 32-bit versus 64-bit addressing, data transfer rates, SQL joins, binary large objects, database indexes, computer hardware upgrades, migrating to new releases, and the latest Dilbert cartoons—all without having to endure the snickers, sidelong looks, and snarky comments of the data center's more mainstream knowledge workers.

"You *do* realize that you are wasting your money, don't you?" a familiar voice boomed at the back of my head.

I turned to see Burton sitting with three of the other systems programmers at the table behind me. He had his trademark *I am a techie god* smirk on his face, and his eyes twinkled from behind Coke-bottle-thick glasses.

"Huh?" I asked. I had just come from one of the vending machines that lined the far wall of the break room, where I had purchased a little brown bag of button-shaped, hard-coated chocolate candies that were famous for melting in your mouth, not in your hand. I was about to sit back down at the table with Dave and Ying, who were finishing their respective lunches.

Burton cocked his head sharply to the left to indicate that I was to look in that direction. I did, and there it was. Standing by the bulletin board was a brand-new vending machine that resembled the gumball machines commonly found beyond grocery store checkout counters. The top of the machine consisted of a clear glass globe with a shiny metal cap on it. The globe sat on a rectangular, cherry-red metal base unit that had a decorative band of silver trim running along the top and another running along the bottom. The front-center of the base unit had a slot where you could insert a quarter, a whale-fluke-like handle that you could twist, and a small chute with a metal flap at the end. The base unit was supported by a three-foot-long black metal pole that was grounded in a round, black metal base. The globe of the machine was filled with the very type of candy that I had just purchased from the vending machine.

Burton was the manager of the Systems Programming Group and reputed to be the smartest person in the data center. He only associated with other systems programmers and with upper management. So, I knew that the only reason he was talking to me was to deride me in some manner or another.

"How many pieces do you think come in one of those little bags?" Burton asked.

"Anywhere from fifty to fifty-five," I replied.

"Oh, so he counts them," Burton swung his head around to his posse with a big grin to show how ridiculous I was. They all laughed, and Peterson, who was his main ass-kisser, laughed the hardest.

"Well," said Burton, getting up from the table, "I'll bet that you can actually get more pieces from that new machine than from the bag, and at a better price."

Burton stood up and walked over to the machine while fishing for change in his left pocket. He was dressed in *sysprog* high couture—loafers, khaki pants, and a blue polo shirt with a major computer company's logo printed on the right breast pocket.

"So, how much did that there little bag set you back?" he asked.

"It cost 75 cents," I answered flatly. I didn't really want to be a part of it, but I was now trapped in his idiot conversation.

"Okay, so this new machine is 25 cents a pop." He counted out two quarters from the handful of coins he had extracted from his pocket. "So, I'll bet that these here two quarters net me more than what is in that 75-cent bag of yours." Behind my back, Peterson snickered his delight.

Burton slid his first quarter into the coin slot. Then he took hold of the machine with both hands and rocked it back and forth, back and forth, back and forth. He put his left hand against the metal door at the end of the chute to keep it from swinging open. Next, he turned the dial with slow deliberate motion. We could hear the click-click-click of the mechanism, followed by the metallic ka-chink of the quarter falling into the money bin, and then the frenetic clatter of the candies falling out of the hopper and plip-plopping down the chute. Burton cupped his right hand beneath the chute and removed his left hand from blocking the metal door. A heap of brown, orange, red, green, yellow, and blue candies cascaded into his right hand.

Burton took the handful of candies over to his table and dumped them in front of Peterson. He returned to the machine, inserted another quarter, got a second handful, and then poured them into the pile in front of Peterson.

"Count 'em!" he instructed. Peterson happily complied.

"Count yours, too," Burton instructed me. Everybody in the break room was quietly waiting to see what would happen, so I had no choice. I ripped open the top of my bag and poured the candies out in front of me. I counted them . . . *two, four, six, eight, ten . . . fifty-three.*

"There were fifty-three in the bag," I announced.

At the other table, I heard Peterson finishing, ". . . sixty, sixty-one, sixty-two. Sixty-two! Hah! Burton's right—nine more pieces. What a waste of money!"

"Let's see," said Burton, continuing to hold court. "What we really have here is the difference between the bag cost and the . . . um . . . the . . . *twist* cost. How much does a bag weigh?" he asked me.

I picked up the empty bag and looked at the weight printed on the front. "1.69 ounces or 47 grams," I read.

"Well, since this is the US of A, we will go with ounces instead of grams," Burton schooled me. "Peterson, divide 1.69 by 53 so that we can get the per piece weight."

Peterson pulled out his iPhone, started the calculator app, and began typing. "So that's 0.031886792452830 ounces per piece of candy," he announced. "Hey, the 1886792452830 is a repeating decimal after the initial .03!"

Burton ignored him and rolled on. "Okay, so we will make that .0318 ounces per piece. Now, multiply .0318 by sixty-two—the number we got in two twists."

"That's 1.9716," Peterson reported.

"1.97 ounces versus 1.69 ounces. Now I would say that is a much better deal!" Burton declared triumphantly.

"Don't forget the cost!" Peterson reminded.

"I was getting to that," Burton chided. Peterson looked chastened. "Divide 50 cents by 62 and then divide 75 cents by 53."

Peterson's eyes narrowed, and he silently mouthed the numbers as he thumb-typed the higher-math calculations. Finally, he looked up and said, "It's 0.8064 cents per candy for the twists and 1.4150 cents per candy for a bag. So, bag candies are 43 percent more expensive than twist candies. Ha, ha. Burton was right!"

"Okay, then," I said. "Can I finish my lunch in peace, now?"

"Yea, sure," said Burton with a big smile. "Case closed!" he declared, sitting back down at the table with his satellites.

"Twists are even more physically economical," Amit piped up from Burton's table. "You see, twists call for two actions—putting the quarter in the slot and then twisting the dial. You do that twice and you have four actions. Contrast that with the machine, where you have to put three quarters in the slot, then push the F-button, then push the 9-button to indicate that you want the bag of candy in the F9 slot. That's five actions for a bag and only four actions for the twists."

Everybody at the system programmers table nodded approvingly at Amit's logic.

"What if I use a dollar bill instead of quarters?" Dave offered up from our table. "Then it's only three actions: putting the dollar bill in the machine, pushing the F-button, and then pushing the 9-button. In that case, it is more physically economical to get a bag than to do the twists."

There was silence for a minute as everybody considered Dave's clever rebuttal.

"Nope, doesn't work," Amit finally said. "The bags cost 75 cents, so you get a quarter in change. You still have to retrieve your quarter. That means you have to swing the change door open and then take the quarter out. That's two actions right there. Add those to the other three and you still have five actions for a bag, as opposed to only four actions for the twists." He smiled proudly at his clever analysis. Burton gave him a fist bump.

"What I want to know," said Mary from the Java programmers' lunch table, ". . . is how many twists you need and how many bags you need in order to get the same gross number of pieces."

"I'm on it!" Ying said. As always, he had brought his laptop to our lunch table and had been working on a project while he had been eating. Ying began to type in furious, exaggerated motions. Dave pushed his chair back, stood up, walked around the table, and looked over Ying's shoulder.

"I don't get the question," Peterson said. "You want to compare *what* to *what*?" He looked around at the other systems programmers to make sure they were in on his question.

Mary signed heavily and rolled her eyes. She and Peterson never got along, and his question was designed more to make her look foolish than to elicit any clarification.

"At some point, the number of pieces you get in a series of twists will equal the number of pieces you get in a group of bags," Mary explained slowly as if talking to a child. "I want to know what that number of pieces is and—more importantly—how many twists and how many bags it takes to get to it. Understand now?"

Peterson just nodded. It was clear that he wasn't going to score any points at Mary's expense in front of his crew.

"Got it!" Ying said. Peterson, Amit, and Mary got up from their seats and joined Dave standing behind Ying, looking at the laptop. Burton stayed seated at his table chewing on an apple with a look of bemusement on his face.

"It's like this," Ying began. "You get 53 pieces in a bag and 31 pieces in a twist. As you add them up, the two separate amounts first intersect when you have 53 twists and 31 bags. The total amount in 53 twists is 1,643 pieces. And the total amount in 31 bags is also 1,643 pieces. So, to answer Mary's question, 53 twists or 31 bags will net you the first same gross number of pieces, which is 1,643 candies."

Dave and I smiled at Ying. *Score one for our table!*

"What's the cost of those 1,643 pieces for the 53 twists and for the 31 bags?" Burton asked. The smile on his face signaled that he was sure the twist cost would be less than the bag cost, further backing up his original point.

"The cost for 53 twists is $13.25," said Ying. "The cost for 31 bags is $23.25. Hey, that's a $10 difference!"

"Told you!" Burton said pointing to me.

"Yeah, he told you so," Peterson echoed.

I looked at the two of them deadpan and didn't respond. *I so wanted out of there!*

"Hmmm . . ." said Ying, "it looks like there are 37 intersections between the amount of candy you get with twists and with bags within the first 2,000 twists. The number of bags and twists intersect at increasing multiples of 53 and 31, respectively." *Now he was just showing off.*

"So, the second intersection is 106 twists and 62 bags for a total of 3,286 pieces in either group. The third intersection is 159 twists and 93 bags for a total of 4,929 pieces in either group. At the 37th intersection, you have 1,961 twists or 1,147 bags, either of which contains 60,791 pieces. The total twist cost would be $490.25, and the total bag cost would be $860.25. The difference would be a whopping $370.00!"

"Whoa!" went a chorus of voices from those looking over Ying's shoulder. Burton laughed a loud *I told you so*, which his toady quickly echoed.

"Yes, but!" Susan's strong, firm, authoritative voice cut through the break room, silencing all side conversations.

Susan, a seriously good C# programmer, was our organization's "yes, but" person. In every meeting she attended, no matter what the subject matter was, no matter how mature the plan being discussed was, she could always be counted on to *yes, but* it. Susan had the uncanny ability of finding the subtle flaws and inconsistencies that everybody else missed. She always followed her *yes, buts* up by pointing out the problems and then laying out clever workarounds to or remediations of the issues. Those who were open to a thorough discussion of a systems initiative invited her to the planning meetings; those with big egos at stake did not.

"There is a basic flaw in your assumptions that is affecting your calculations," she continued. She paused to take in the two-dozen pairs of eyes that were locked onto her.

"Well, please *do* enlighten us," Burton said sarcastically.

"I'm about to do just that," Susan said with a sly smile. She had *yes, butted* Burton in several meetings, and there was no love lost between the two of them.

"You are all operating under a false premise. Burton dumped two twists worth of candies in front of Peterson. Peterson counted 62 pieces and everybody assumed that it was 31 per twist."

"So?" asked Burton, trying to dismiss her, though it was pretty clear where she was going.

"So, we don't really know if the first twist netted 30 and the second twist netted 32." Susan continued. "Or if the first twist produced 28 and the second twist produced 34. In short; we don't have a reliable number for the pieces you get in a twist."

"But there were two twists and we ended up with 62 pieces," Peterson butted in, defending his boss. "Can't we just assume that it is 31 pieces in each twist?" The rest of us, including Burton, saw the flaw in his logic and stayed silent.

"Nope," said Susan. "That is not necessarily true. And even it was—even if we did get 31 per twist—an N of 2 is way too small a sample size. We need many, many more observations in order to approach the real number of candies in a twist."

"How many?" Peterson challenged.

"Depends," Susan replied, not taking the bait.

"We would also have to do the same thing with the bags," Dave interjected.

"Exactly!" Susan exclaimed, triumphantly. "I was just about to go there. Michael originally replied that there were anywhere from fifty to fifty-five pieces per bag. The fact that he counted 53 from that one bag doesn't establish it as the official count of candies per bag. It only establishes 53 as the number of candies in *that* bag." She paused to be sure we were all following her before plunging on.

"We should determine an N for twists and for bags and then take the average yield of each as our representative numbers. Then we can have Ying recalculate the yields and costs."

"How about 100?" Peterson asked. "The average count in 100 twists versus the average count in 100 bags."

"Okay," said Susan with a sly smile. "Only trouble is: who will buy a bag now, knowing that two twists are a better deal?"

I looked around me to see that everybody was nodding their assent. She had nailed both the problem and the new dilemma.

"Well, I'm going start the count right now by getting me a twist or two," Peterson said heading over to the machine. Amit and Henry followed him, as did three or four non-sysprogs. A line quickly formed in front of the shiny red vending machine. A rapid succession of noises descended upon the break room: the click-click-click of the coin mechanism, followed by the metallic ka-chink of quarters falling into the money bin, followed by clatter of the candies plip-plopping down the chute, and ending with exclamations such as *Hey, I got 33!* or *Darn—I only got 29!*

"I'm out of here," I told Ying and Dave. I scooped up my overpriced candies, dumped them into my reusable cloth lunch bag, crumbled my foil sandwich wrapper up around my empty chip bag, and grabbed my nearly empty bottle of water. Dave and Ying likewise cleaned up their lunchtime debris, and the three of us stopped by the trash and recycling bins before heading out.

"Man, I'm glad that's over," I said to my companions as we headed out of the break room. Ying and Dave both laughed.

But it was *not* over. Not at all. That was just the end of the beginning.

*****

The next day, I arrived at Techie Lunch Hour 15 minutes late due to a dull noontime staff meeting that had overrun its time slot. The moment that I entered the break room, I could feel the excitement in the air. A group of people were crowded around the sysprog's table looking down at something and discussing it. The whole room was buzzing with lively conversations.

"What's up?" I asked Ying and Dave as I plopped my lunch bag and bottled water down in my customary spot between them.

"Two things," said Dave. "Peterson got a fractional piece of candy in a twist and they are arguing over whether or not to count it. And Burton wants to know how many candies the machine can hold. So, Amit went to get a tape measure. I think he's going to measure the circumference of the machine's globe, or its radius, or something."

"Jeez, it's still going, eh?" I said, pulling out my chair and sitting down.

"Yup," said Ying from behind his laptop. "And I see that there is half the amount of candy in the machine today as there was at this time yesterday. That machine is pretty popular."

I noted that Ying was right as I took a sandwich, an apple, and a bag of corn chips out of my lunch bag. I also noted that the discussion from the sysprog table was getting louder. Curiosity got the better of me, so I got up and walked over to the group standing around the table.

Looking over Mary's shoulder, I could see Burton, Ed, and Peterson sitting at the table. In front of Peterson was a malformed, partial piece of candy. He was turning it over and over, and rotating it this way and that way so that everybody could see its dimensions. The group was staring at the candy fragment with the same intensity they would have given to the red and blue wire connections on a ticking time bomb, the hanging chad on a paper ballot, or a hexadecimal data dump.

"I still say that we shouldn't count it at all," Peterson urged the group.

"Well, like I said: you can't just pretend that you didn't get it in a twist," Mary argued.

"No, but I don't think that we really want to get into fractions here," Ed retorted, backing up his fellow sysprog.

Ed glanced up and spotted me standing behind Mary.

"We are not likely to get partial candies in a bag. Right, Michael?" he asked. "You've never had partial candies in a bag, have you?"

"Um, yeah, sure, no, whatever," I replied.

"See!" Ed asserted, using my somewhat less than firm affirmation as solid evidence. "If we don't have partials in a bag, we shouldn't count them in a twist."

"But you *cannot* just ignore them. It's inexact!" Mary stated, exasperated. "You wouldn't be so imprecise applying patches to your mainframe's operating system. So, why would you be inexact here?"

"Compromise!" Burton declared in a loud voice. "This is what we are going to do: we are going to follow the normal rules of rounding off numbers. When a piece is less than half, we will *round down* and not count it at all. When a piece is half or greater, then we will *round up* and count it."

"But . . . ," Ed started.

"End of story!" Burton said loudly, giving Ed a laser-hot look of authority.

Ed sighed and looked away.

Mary shook her head and looked away, too. It was obvious that she was not satisfied. But she was smart enough not to argue the point with Burton.

With the drama over counting fragments concluded, I walked back to my table and joined Ying and Dave. I unwrapped my sandwich, spread the foil wrapper out on the table, and placed my sandwich squarely in the middle of the wrapper. I popped open the top of my bag of corn chips, ripped it down one side, spread the bag open, and put it in the three o'clock position next to my sandwich wrapper. Then I twisted the cap off of my bottled water and placed it in the nine o'clock position next to my sandwich wrapper. Lunch was served!

Just as I picked up my sandwich, Amit sprinted into the break room with a yellow cloth tape measure hanging from his right hand. "Got it," he said striding directly over to the candy machine. Peterson, Mary, and Ed joined him at the machine.

Amit adjusted the tape measure so that the side with the inch markings was facing outward. He secured one end of the tape measure under his right thumb against the glass globe. Then he stretched the tape measure around the middle of the globe with his left hand. When the tape measure overlapped where his thumb was, he pulled it tight and leaned in to record the measure. Peterson, Mary, and Ed leaned in, too.

"Okay," said Amit, "I get 31 inches and about 3/8 of an inch. Let's see, as a decimal, 3/8 of an inch is about . . ."

".375 inches," Ying shot over from our table.

"Right. Then, for argument's sake, let's round that up to .4 inches. So, we will say that the globe's circumference is 31.4 inches total. Okay?" Amit scanned the assembly for consensus.

Several people nodded their assent, and several murmured, "Yes." So, the globe's circumference was officially accepted as being 31.4 inches.

"Let's do this!" Amit said excitedly with a gleam in his eyes. "To get the volume of the candy machine's globe, we first have to determine the globe's radius. Peterson, do you have your calculator ready?"

"Yup," Peterson said standing up and waiving his iPhone in Amit's direction.

"So, the formula for deriving the radius from the circumference is: $R = C / 2\pi$. Now, we have 31.4 divided by two times 3.14; which is 31.4 divided by 6.28. What's that?"

"It's 5," said Peterson, "or rather: it's 5 inches."

"Wait," said Dave. "You are using a very simplistic value of π when you use 3.14. That's the 'schoolkid' version of π. You should be using something like 3.14159 or more. That will give you greater precision."

"No, we are only going to use 3.14 for π," Amit retorted. "It will simplify the calculations, and since this is not a programming issue, we are not necessarily going for maximum precision."

"Fine," said Dave. I could see that it wasn't really fine with him, but he didn't want to argue the point any further.

"Okay, so where was I?" Amit asked rhetorically. "Oh, right! So, the radius of the globe is 5 inches. We calculate volume as: Volume = 4/3 * π * R^3. So, Peterson, that would be 4/3 times 3.14 times 5-cubed. Got it?"

"Uh . . . ," Peterson said thumb-typing into his iPhone. "That's 4/3 times 3.14. And then multiply it by 5-to-the-third-power. Okay, I've got 523.33 cubic inches."

"Nice!" said Amit. "So, the volume of the globe is 523.33 cubic inches. Now, we need to determine the volume of a single piece of candy and multiply it times the volume of the globe. That will get us the number of pieces in the globe."

"How are we going to do that?" asked Peterson. "The candies are so small."

"Got it!" said Ying from our table. "I just looked it up on the web. The volume of a single piece of this candy is .0215 fluid ounces."

"Perfect!" Amit exclaimed. "Peterson, divide 523.33 by .0215."

"Whoa, not so fast!" Ying interjected. "We have two issues here that we need to work out."

"What?" Peterson and Amit both asked at the same time.

"First, I can only find the volume of a piece of that candy in *fluid ounces*. We determined the volume of the globe in *cubic inches*. Fluid ounces versus cubic inches! Those are two incompatible measures. So, we need to first translate the 523.33 cubic inches into fluid ounces."

"And how do we do that?" asked Amit, clearly annoyed at being out-thought on the calculation and losing the floor to Ying.

"I'm looking that up now," Ying said distractedly. "Ah! So, the formula for doing that is Volume in Fluid Ounces = Volume in Cubic Inches / 1.8046875."

"Peterson, divide 523.33 by 1.8046875," Ying instructed.

I saw Peterson look first to Amit and then to Burton. He didn't want to take directions from a non-systems programmer. Burton nodded his head in consent, and Peterson started typing.

"Dividing 523.33 by 1.8046875 gets you 289.983723," Peterson reported.

"That's 289.983723 fluid ounces in the globe," Ying clarified. "Let's round that back to four decimal places so that we have 289.9837 fluid ounces in the globe."

"So, now we divide that by the volume of a single piece of candy," said Amit authoritatively; trying to wrestle back control of the conversation.

"Nope!" said Ying.

"Nope, why?" demanded Amit.

"I originally said that there were *two* issues," said Ying. "We only took care of issue number one."

"Well, will you *please* enlighten us as to nature of the remaining issue?" asked Burton. He was on his way over to our table.

"Yeah, sure. We need to account for the *random packing ratio* of the candies," Ying continued unfazed.

"The *random what* issue?" Peterson snorted in a ridiculing tone.

"The random packing ratio," said Ying. "When solid objects are dumped into a container, they have some amount of space left between them. This happens even when you shake the container to help them settle into their tightest level of packing. Thus, solid objects cannot fill the entire volume of their containers. You account for the unused space by using the random packing ratio."

"You're kidding," said Peterson, rolling his eyes. "Where did you get that idea?"

"No, I'm not kidding," said Ying. "It's a common factor that is used in the classic math problem of determining how many spheres can be packed into a container." Ying had been a math major in college.

"Okay, so . . . um . . . ," Amit said, clearly out of his depth.

"So, the random packing ratio for these candies is .685," said Ying, reading from his laptop. "And the formula for determining how many candies fit into that globe now becomes Number of Candies = Volume of the Sphere * (Random Packing Ratio / Volume of a Single Candy).

"Peterson, multiply 289.9837 times .685. Then divide by .0215."

"That comes out to 9239.0155581," Peterson said. "So rounding it, you can have 9,239 pieces of candy in that globe."

"Hmm . . . ," said Ying, typing on his laptop. "At 31 pieces per twist, there are approximately 298 twists in that machine. And, at 25-cents a twist, the vendor will make $74.50 from a single globe's-worth." *Ying was clearly showing off again.*

An excited murmur went through the break room as everybody digested the latest facts. So many twists. So much money.

"Yes, but!" Susan's voice cut through the break room.

"Oh, jeez. What now?" Burton exclaimed rolling his eyes. We all turned to see that Susan was standing up at her table.

"'*What now*' is that there are more bugs in these calculations than in the first release of a software package, that's what," Susan replied.

Burton goaded her: "Such as . . ."

"Such as the uneven rounding that was done, for starters," Susan answered. "Sometimes decimal places were rounded to two places, sometimes to four places, and sometimes they were simply truncated."

"Then there is the problem with the number of pieces in a twist. Ying used 31 as the value. But, yesterday, we all decided that we need to establish an accepted value for the number of pieces in a twist. That has not been done yet."

"Okay," said Burton, "those are two small things."

"Mm-hmm . . . ," said Susan with a gleam in her eye. "But the biggest issue of all concerns the assumptions about the container itself—the globe!"

Susan walked around her table, past the sysprog's table, past the small group at my table, and stopped in front of the machine. All eyes were on her, and the room was completely silent.

"You will notice that there is silver metal cap atop of the globe where the vendor dumps the candy in," she said, touching it with her right hand. "That means that the very top of the globe is not completely round. The cap area adds some volume to the top of this candy machine. So, candies could fill up that additional cap area."

"Also, as you can see, there is a round hole in the bottom of the globe where it fits into the base." Susan pointed to that area of the candy machine. "That's where the candy wheel and hopper mechanisms are located. There is room for additional candies in the base of the unit, beneath the bottom of the globe. From here, it looks like there is an inch or two of space in the base of the candy machine."

"Meaning?" asked Burton, impatiently taking the bait.

"Meaning that Ying didn't take those areas into account in his calculations. There is actually more volume in that machine than the simple computation of the volume of the globe yielded. So, Ying's calculations are invalid," Susan concluded.

"Can't we just assume that the vendor doesn't fill the globe to the very top and that Ying's calculation is relatively correct?" Peterson asked. It was clear that his lame attempt to defend his boss was going to quickly go down in flames.

"Well, you can assume anything that you want," Susan retorted. "I don't know how you conduct business in the Systems Programming Group, but in the Web Programmers Group we avoid assumptions and program for maximum precision."

Susan's triumphant smile was as rewarding to see as was Peterson's look of exasperation.

"Twist time!" Burton called out, jingling a couple of quarters in his hand. He and Susan passed each other on their respective ways to and from the candy machine.

A line quickly formed behind Burton and soon the break room was again filled with the sounds of the click-click-click of the coin mechanism, followed by the metallic ka-chink of quarters falling into the money bin, followed by the clattering of candies plip-plopping down the chute, and ending with various exclamations and discussions about the candy yields.

*****

In the following weeks, the candy machine became a hot topic of conversation both in and out of the break room. We talked about the twist counts, how much money the vendor was making, how many twists you could do in an hour if there were to be an infinite supply of candy in the machine, the likely candy volume of the *entire* machine, the best way to shake the machine in order to get the most candies, whether or not counting fractions of a candy was really a good idea, the likely cost to the vendor of buying the candy in bulk, whether we should keep track of the ratio of the various colors of the candies to one another, how the vendor could double profits by installing a second machine, how frustrating it was that the machine ran out of candy by the end of the week, and a host of other important issues.

The candy machine also became a popular social destination for techies to visit throughout the day. It was not uncommon for Dave or Ying to look up from their PC workstations mid-afternoon and say something like: *My brain is fried—I'm heading downstairs for a twist*. Likewise, colleagues would poke their heads into our office and say: *Hey, I'm headed to the break room for a twist. Want to come?* It even became an acceptable excuse for arriving late to data center meetings: *Sorry we're late; we stopped for a twist on the way over*. And when you did go to the break room, you would usually find a group of programmers sitting around a table with a couple of quarters' worth of the brown, orange, red, green, yellow, and blue candies spread out in front of them.

We tried to keep track of the highest twist count by posting it on a yellow sticky note on the side of the machine. But some unknown person kept removing it. Late one Tuesday afternoon, Dave chanced upon a vending company worker who had come in to refill the machines. He saw the man peel off the sticky note and throw it into a trashcan. Dave asked him why he had done it. The worker replied that it was the vending company's policy to only allow "Out of Order" signs to be posted on their machines. All other postings had to be removed. Dave explained the concept of the twist count and the importance of our keeping track of the highest number. The worker gave Dave a blank stare during his explanation. Then he said: *I don't know about all that. I only know that it's company policy not to have anything other than "Out of Order" signs on the machines.*

After Dave's encounter, we kept the twist count on an index card tacked to the break room's bulletin board. But then some joker kept writing down famous large numbers like 92,955,807 and 1,073,741,824 and 10^{80} on the index card when nobody was in the break room. Some suspected that it was one of the security guards since it seemed to be happening during off hours. But most of us suspected that one of the non-programming data center staff members was doing it to spoof us.

Raul, one of the SQL Server database administrators, got the highest official twist count of 35 pieces of candy. Though one could easily have misconstrued Raul's high twist count as being blind luck, he apparently considered it to be an example of his prowess. He was often heard describing in excruciating detail exactly how he had rocked the machine back and forth seven times, inserted the quarter with the tails-side outward, twisted the dial one click per second while vibrating the machine with his left hand, and then giving the machine a sharp shove at the exact moment that he heard the candies being released. The systems programmers were particularly vocal about ridiculing Raul's elaborate story. But I actually saw Ed trying to duplicate Raul's technique one afternoon when the break room was empty and he didn't hear me come in. He spotted me when he was counting his haul and sheepishly reported that he had only netted 29.

Despite our best intentions, we never did establish an official N for either the twist count or the bag count. Amit had posted a sign-up sheet on the bulletin board for people to enter the date, their twist count or bag count, and their initials. People were pretty diligent about updating the twist count at first, so we had high hopes of getting to 100 samples relatively quickly. But, after the second week, people only sporadically updated the twist count column with what their precious quarters had yielded. The bag count suffered a somewhat similar fate. Since everybody was wise to the fact that twists were more economical than bags, there were only three entries in the bag count column. After a month, the sign-up sheet was taken down to make room for an order form for the Girl Scout cookie drive. Nobody missed it, and nobody complained.

*****

Late one afternoon, Dave burst into the office that he, Ying, Karen, and I shared.

"It's gone!" he exclaimed breathlessly.

"What's gone?" I asked.

"The candy machine," he replied. "They took it away."

"What?" Ying and I and Karen all exclaimed. "Why?" I asked.

"The data center changed concession vendors," said Dave. "The old vendor removed all of their machines about an hour ago, and the new vendor just moved in the new machines. Our candy machine left with the old vendor."

"Wow," said Ying.

"Bummer," I said, dejectedly.

"Yeah, bummer," Dave sadly agreed.

Karen never ate sweets, so she didn't reply outright. She just snorted her amusement and went back to the program she was working on.

The loss of the candy machine cast a pall over Techie Lunch Hour, and its previous insular social environment returned. There were conversations at the mainframe systems programmers' table, the UNIX administrators' table, the Java programmers' table, the computer performance analysts' table, the web programmers' table, and the database administrators' table—but not between the tables anymore. Gone were the spirited, good-humored group discussions and arguments about the various facets of twists and yields and bags of candies. They were replaced by the tried-and-true conversations about bits and bytes, memory registers, 32- versus 64-bit addressing, data transfer rates, SQL joins, binary large objects, database indexes, computer hardware upgrades, migrating to new releases, and the latest Dilbert cartoons. Though these were all very interesting topics, they just didn't have quite the same magic that had surrounded our conversations about the candy machine.

The spot where the candy machine had stood looked empty and forlorn. We missed the sight of the shiny red base atop of the long black pole, and the globe with its precious cargo of brown, orange, red, green, yellow, and blue candies, all ready to be ours for only a quarter's investment and a quick twist. We missed the rowdy lines of programming nerds that formed in front of the machine at the end of Techie Lunch Hour. We missed the click-click-click of the coin mechanism, the metallic ka-chink of quarters falling into the money bin, and the clattering of the candies plip-plopping down the chute. We missed the exclamations of people getting a successful twist count and the oaths of those who were stiffed by the machine.

But, eventually, the old normal became the new normal once again, and we forgot all about those exciting few months.

*****

"You *do* realize that you are wasting your money, don't you?" a familiar voice boomed at the back of my head.

I turned to see Burton sitting with three of the other systems programmers at the table behind me. He had his trademark *I am a techie god* smirk on his face, and his eyes twinkled from behind Coke-bottle-thick glasses.

"Huh?" I asked. I had just come from one of the vending machines that lined the far wall of the break room where I had purchased a little clear bag of salted peanuts that were famous for the cartoon mascot who sported a top hat and a monocle and carried a cane. I was about to sit back down at the table with Dave and Ying, who were finishing their respective lunches.

Burton cocked his head sharply to the left to indicate that I was to look in that direction. I did, and there it was. Standing by the bulletin board was a brand new vending machine that resembled the gumball machines commonly found beyond grocery store checkout counters. The top of the machine consisted of a clear glass globe with a shiny metal cap on it. The globe sat on a rectangular, cherry-red metal base unit that had a decorative band of silver trim running along the top and another along the bottom. The front-center of the base unit had a slot where you could insert a quarter, a whale-fluke-like handle that you could twist, and a small chute with a metal flap at the end. The base unit was supported by a three-foot-long black metal pole that was grounded in a round, black metal base. The globe of the machine was filled with the type of salted peanuts that I had just purchased from the vending machine.

"Oh, no!" Dave lamented. "Not again!"

"Infinite loop!" Ying quipped, shaking his head and getting his laptop ready.

1111 HAPPY TRAILS TO ME

Everybody knows that there is no such thing as a *secret* in a large office. Benjamin Franklin is credited with writing "Three may keep a secret, if two of them are dead." In that particular office, a mass extinction would have had to take place for any secret to be kept. People held impromptu conversations over the cubicle walls, in the hallways, around the water cooler, in the coffee break area, outside the restrooms, inside the restrooms, in the copier room, outside the elevators, inside the elevators, outside the cafeteria, inside the cafeteria, and on their telephones. They talked about office politics, Peggy's hair styles, sports events, Peggy's loud dresses, commuting woes, Peggy's flashy shoes, weather conditions, Peggy's exotic vacations, national politics, who Peggy was dating, their weekend plans, Peggy's weekend plans, and more. Nobody seemed to filter their thoughts, lower their voices, or moderate their conversations according to who was standing or sitting nearby. So, it was inevitable that I found out about my surprise going-away party.

I found out about my surprise party three different ways. First, I found a printed flyer for the party that was unintentionally left on one of the machines in the copier room. Next, I was accidentally *carbon copied* on an email that discussed a programming issue, but had a reference to catching up at "Michael's going-away party." Finally, I overheard snatches of one of Peggy's telephone conversations from her cubicle across the hallway: "Michael . . ." ". . . surprise party . . ." "Friday . . ." ". . . noon . . ." Consequently, I understood why Peggy had sent me an invitation for a *debriefing meeting* in the large conference room on the fifth floor at noontime on my last day with the organization. You didn't have to be a Sherlock Holmes in that office; the clues came looking for you on their own.

I had very mixed emotions about leaving that organization. On the one hand, I was very excited. I had found a job at a company that I had known about for years and had always dreamed of working for one day. They highly valued the programming skill set that I possessed, and my prospects were very good for a long and rewarding career there. But I had loved the organization I was leaving. I loved their mission, their sophisticated computer systems, the challenging programming work, and the great feeling of accomplishment I got when we finished a big project. The problem was that the organization did not love me back.

My career there had stalled out after five years of solid, satisfying programming work. Every year, I got positive reviews, good raises, and a few letters of recognition from happy internal clients. But, try as I might, I could not seem to get myself promoted. I made no secret of the fact that I was ready to take on more responsibilities and wanted to become a manager. I had a growing family at the time and making more money was important to me. But my inquiries and entreaties fell upon the ears of apathetic management. The event that finally precipitated my departure was the first annual performance review that Logan conducted.

Logan had taken over as our acting associate director when Mr. Spellings had retired. Logan was a career bureaucrat who had risen to his highest level of incompetence within the organization. Over the years, he had consistently failed as associate director for a number of other groups in the organization and had been shuffled around numerous times. Because he carpooled into the city with two of the assistant vice presidents and played golf with them on weekends, he was safe from ever being let go. Since our group was pretty well self-directed and did not need a lot of supervision, Logan had found a safe haven "managing" us. He could come in late, read the *Washington Post* in his office, take long lunches, and leave early whenever he wanted to.

Soon after Logan arrived, I realized that he had taken a disliking to me. The first sign of it was when Logan pointedly ignored me in the hallways. He would look right through me and not respond when I said hello in the morning. If I was with somebody, he would acknowledge them, but ignore me. He thought nothing of interrupting a conversation I was having with another team member to talk to them, acting as if I wasn't there at all. It didn't matter whether I was having a technical discussion with a colleague or not; when he wanted to say something, he butted in and said something.

Logan's dislike next began surfacing in email messages that I carbon copied him on in order to keep him in the loop since he was my boss. He would fire back a response with a series of sharp questions even though it was a technical discussion between programmers. The fact that he didn't understand very much about programming made it very frustrating because I had to write back lengthy explanations of what we were talking about and why we were taking a particular course of action. He would follow up with additional email messages either debating points that I had made or making idiot suggestions for alternative courses of action. I quickly learned not to copy him on any of my correspondences.

Logan also made a habit of shooting down anything that I said in the marathon Friday morning staff meetings that he held. If I was explaining something, he would find some nuanced way to "correct" me. If I asked a question, he would act as if the answer was obvious and give me a very condescending answer. If I made a suggestion to one of the other staff members during a discussion, he would quickly butt in and explain why it could not possibly work. His knee-jerk reaction to anything that I said in public was so obvious that even Peggy commented on it. "Ooh, Logan really doesn't like *you*," she said with a smile one Friday as we poured out of the meeting.

When I entered Logan's office for my annual review, I was not sure how it would go. He had been my boss for only about six months, and I did not know how invested he had been in really keeping track of what I had been doing. I should have realized, though, that it would not go well for me. I normally got the top rating of "Very Good" for my four Competency Areas: Job Knowledge, Technical Skills, Professional Application, and Working with Others. But he had marked me as "Good" for all of the ratings. It was like going from earning straight A's to all B's.

"What?" I asked Logan. "How could I possibly have only earned 'Goods' when I always get 'Very Goods' for my ratings?"

"That's what you got," Logan said. He had been gazing at me from across his desk with his arms crossed, his head cocked sideways, and a slight smile on his face. Now he traded one body language power pose for another by leaning back in his chair, putting his hands behind his head, and staring me down. He had obviously done well in his Upper Management 201 class.

"No way!" I said. "This year, I created two computer systems that are now being used in all of our offices throughout the United States. I arranged for our team to be interviewed and featured in two articles for the computer weekly that covers our industry. The Chief Information Officer came down to *my* cubicle to get a first-hand demonstration of one of the new computer systems. And the other new system was nominated for a prestigious national award. So, how can I possibly only get 'Goods' for my ratings?"

Logan let a minute pass before answering just to make sure that I knew he was fully in charge. "It's your attitude," he finally said.

"My attitude? What's wrong with my attitude?" I asked incredulously.

"You don't take your work seriously. You joke your way around the office. Everything is just fun and games to you."

"There's nothing wrong with my *attitude*; I get things done. My accomplishments speak for themselves. And that's how it should be. You should be judging me for the work that I get done, not for whether or not I pass some half-assed personality test of yours."

"Watch it," Logan warned, his tone becoming deadly serious, his face becoming dark.

I realized that I was dangerously close to giving him the very reaction that he wanted, the reaction that could give him an actual grievance against me. No—I was too smart for that.

"Is that all?" I asked sharply.

"Yes, that's all. Just sign the bottom of your review, and we are through," Logan said with a condescending smile.

I signed his copy, took my copy, and stormed out of his office. We were not through, not through at all! I marched back to my cubicle, logged into my PC, and made an appointment to talk to Mr. Trowel, Logan's boss. There are always dangers to lodging a complaint with your boss's boss. Managers usually back up the decisions of other managers—that must be one of the first things that they teach in management school. But I didn't think that I had anything to lose at that point. It was my last ditch effort to salvage my career with the organization, my last chance to make things right.

Mr. Trowel saw me at the end of the week. Like Logan, he was a lifer bureaucrat in the organization. But, unlike Logan, he was a savvy workaholic who actually drove the people in his division hard and got things done.

"So, you wanted to talk to me about your review and your future in this organization," he began in his stern, no-nonsense voice. Mr. Trowel was a very large, beefy man with a ruddy complexion, a crown of black hair rimmed halfway around his balding head, and a neatly trimmed cop's moustache. He was, as always, impeccably dressed in an expensive suit. The walls of his office were covered with numerous awards he had garnered both within the organization and from industry-related groups.

"Yes. I have had a lot of solid accomplishments this year, and I don't believe that my review ratings accurately reflect them," I explained. "I think that because Logan joined our organization late in the year, he did not have enough time to adequately assess my work."

"I talked to Logan about your case," he said. "We reviewed your accomplishments, and you will be glad to hear that we revised your ratings. You now have 'Very Good' in all of your categories. Okay?" I could see that he had a copy of my review on his desk.

Mr. Trowel handed me the revised copy of my review. I thumbed through it and saw that the categories had been changed as per what he had just stated. He started to shuffle through some papers on his desk, and I realized that he might think we were done. We were not.

"Thank you, Mr. Trowel," I said, "but it is more than just this one review. I have been working for this organization for five years now, doing good work, and I have not been promoted. Not once. Because of my accomplishments, I feel like I should be on some kind of fast track or be near the top of a list of people being considered for promotion."

Mr. Trowel nodded his head slowly, wisely, knowingly. He smiled pleasantly and leaned forward to show me that he was very engaged in our little conversation. He widened his eyes to look friendlier.

"I fully understand. You have done a number of good things

this year. They are all important things, things that are helping our organization move forward. And your work has not gone unnoticed. No, not at all! If you keep up the good work at this same level, then you will be a good candidate for a promotion next year," he lied. "Understand?"

"Yes," I said, "I understand." And I really, really did. Two major computer systems, two articles in a computer weekly, a special visit by the Chief Information Officer, and a nomination for an award were not enough to get me promoted. That level of accomplishment was just not sustainable. I couldn't hope to have two banner years in a row. There were no promotions in my future, especially with Logan there to nip at my heels. My career with the organization was permanently becalmed.

The next few weeks were a blur of out-of-the-office activity. I revised my résumé, did some networking, interviewed with three companies, turned down two offers, and secured a nice job with a tidy salary increase at a great company. My programming skills were actually in demand, and the job search had gone much smoother than I had imagined it would.

After I sent the acceptance letter to my new company, I sat down at my home computer and wrote a resignation letter to my current organization. It was five pages long and listed all of the slights, all of the frustrations, all of the missed opportunities that I had experienced. I wrote about the problems with the organization and how they could be fixed. When I was done, I printed the resignation letter on my home printer and read it out loud with great feeling. I smiled over my own perceived eloquence and how I was *sticking it to the man* with my clever characterizations of what was wrong. Then I put that resignation letter in a folder in the file drawer of my desk and wrote a sparse, formal, two-paragraph resignation letter. That was the letter that I would really submit to the organization. Catharsis was one thing—permanently burning bridges was quite another!

I didn't bother to drop by Logan's office and hand him my resignation letter in person. I emailed it to him, instead. He sent back a terse reply, and I began counting down my final two weeks.

On Wednesday of the second week, I found out about my going-away party three different ways because nobody could keep a secret in that office. I would probably have found out about the party sooner except for two reasons. First, I was slammed with work during those last two weeks. I was finishing hot projects, turning over my programs to Graham, and filling out exit paperwork. Second, I had long ago learned to tune out most of the background chatter in the office, much the same way that you tune out music in grocery stores, highway sounds near the freeway, and your significant other's entreaties for you to stop watching the game and do some work around the house.

I got my *big idea* riding home on the subway Thursday evening. I was thinking about my going-away party and the likelihood that I would be asked to say a few parting words. I didn't want to say something tried and true like "The thing that I will miss most about this job is the people." Or "I've grown a lot in the past few years thanks to all of you." Or "I will never forget my time here in this office." You know, crap like that. I wanted to say something original, something that people would not forget. *Better to burn out than to fade away.* And the idea for the Farewell Luncheon goodbye speech came to me.

After dinner, I squirrelled myself away in my home office and started pounding it out on my PC. I worked on the speech for several hours, constantly revising it, reading it out loud to see if it sounded right, and rewriting portions of it that did not quite work. Around midnight, I was finally satisfied with the speech and printed out two copies on my home printer. I annotated one copy with notes and kept the other one pristine so that I could make copies to pass out. I put both in a Manila folder and placed it on the kitchen table near my keys so that I would remember to bring it to work in the morning.

"Don't forget that we have a mandatory debriefing meeting at noon today," Peggy called out to me as I passed her cubicle on the way to mine that Friday morning. I saw that she was wearing one of her very colorful outfits.

"Nope, I'll be there," I said.

"I'll drop by and pick you up at 11:50," she said. "We will go upstairs together."

"Sure," I said, "11:50." I wondered if she really believed that I was naïve enough to not know what was going to happen. Maybe yes; maybe no.

After dropping my jacket and lunch bag off in my cubicle, I went to the copier and made twenty-five copies of my speech. I tucked them into the folder and was careful not to leave the original on the copier. I did not want to give away my particular secret *that* way.

My last morning turned out to be very, very busy. I had to fill out a lengthy exit interview form, meet with several colleagues to brief them on the current status of various projects, and answer last-minute email messages. I had a deadly deadline of noontime when my computer user ID would be suspended forever since I was leaving. Between other tasks, I emptied my file drawers, relegating some paper to the recycle bin, some to the trashcan, and some to the shredder. I also worked on filling an empty printer paper box with some of my personal items—clock, family pictures, coffee mug, and desk knickknacks.

Suddenly, Peggy was at my cubicle door. "It's 11:57," she said. "We've got to go now."

Peggy and I went down the main corridor and out into the hallway. We walked to the elevators, and she pressed the Up button. The elevators took a few minutes, as they always did, but we were soon on our way up. We emerged on the fifth floor, entered the office area, and started down the main cubicle thoroughfare that led to the big conference room. Peggy made small talk during our little journey. Again, I wondered if she really believed that I was naïve enough to not know what was going to happen. Maybe yes; maybe no.

When we got to the conference room, Peggy opened the door, stepped aside, and let me enter first. The big room was overflowing with people. People were sitting in all of the chairs and crowded two-deep around the long conference table. Practically everybody that I had ever worked with during my five years at the company was there, including some from my old Data Center days. There were also a half-dozen-or-so people that I didn't know, including the two well-dressed women who crashed every retirement, promotion, and going-away party in the organization.

The center of the conference table held a large party platter of cold cuts and cheeses, bowls of salsa and chips, a veggie platter with dips, paper plates, festive napkins, and plastic ware. On a side table there were cans of soda, a large container of ice, and Styrofoam cups. Somebody — probably Peggy — had written *Happy Trails, Michael!* in enormous red, green, and blue letters on the large dry-board behind the side table. I noted that there were two gift-wrapped packages in front of where Peggy was now sitting at the conference table. *All right!*

"Surprise!" a chorus of happy voices shouted.

"Oh wow, you shouldn't have!" I acted surprised.

"You sit right here, short timer," Peggy directed, pulling back the lone empty chair at the head of the table. I sat down.

"Let's not be shy," said Big Bob, grabbing a plate and a plastic fork. "I'm hungry. Let's dig in!"

A happy murmur of agreement rose from the crowd, and people began to attack the food. Two dozen different conversations started as people caught up with one another, trading hellos and work stories. Now and then, people stopped by to ask me who I would be working for or to congratulate me on my new job. Everybody was happy and friendly and cheerful and having a great time. Everybody, that is, except Logan. He only talked to Peggy. He didn't say a word to me. He didn't even make eye contact. *Yeah, big loss!*

About a half-hour into the party, Peggy cleared her throat and stepped in behind me.

"Can I have your attention, everybody? Hello! Everybody! Can I have your attention, please?" Since it was Peggy talking, the room quickly quieted down.

"Good! Before we get to the *Gift Giving* part of Michael's going-away party, we are going to embarrass him with the *Speech Giving* part." She smiled broadly to a chorus of light laughter. "How about a few parting words, Michael?"

"Well," I said. "I kind of knew that this request was coming. And I know that I am not much of a public speaker. So, I did an Internet search and found a company that specializes in speeches for professional occasions."

I looked up to see that I had everybody's rapt attention. This was not normal, and they didn't have a clue as to where I was going.

"I purchased a copy of their Farewell Luncheon speech for today's party. I am going to pass out copies so that you can follow along when I give the speech," I said.

I opened the folder and divided the twenty-five handout copies of the speech into two piles. Then I passed one pile to Peggy who was on my right and one to Big Bob who was sitting on my left. They each took a copy and passed the pile on to the next person.

I waited until all of the copies had been passed out. We were short by about a dozen sheets and I saw some people looking over their neighbors' shoulders. Several people snickered as they previewed the handout. Several laughed out loud. A couple of people pointed to different lines on their copies and read them to their neighbors, who, in turn, smiled. *Nice!*

I waited about two minutes so that everybody would have a chance to read their handout. This is what was on it:

ACME Speech Company

Speech Number 235: Farewell Luncheon

(Act surprised, stand up, clear throat, begin talking in a clear voice).

Well, this is a surprise! I have been with _____ for _____ very _____ years. In that time, I have _____ and _____ a lot of _____ people. Some of the people were real _____, others were very _____ to work with and made me _____. But, on the whole, I think most people at _____ are pretty _____ and full of _____. Overall, I never worked with a group of _____ who were more _____.

(Remember to speak clearly and use expansive gestures).

I will be very _____ to leave _____. And I know all of you will be _____ to see me leave. It will be _____ for the company to fill my position because it is _____ to find somebody who knows his _____ from a _____ in the _____. When they do find some _____ to take my place, please treat that person with the same amount of _____ that you treated me. Remember, that person will have a very _____ job and will need all of the _____ s/he can get. Overall, treat the new _____ as you would have treated me, but don't end up _____ his _____.

(If you are still nervous, imagine your audience is in their underwear).

It's been my pleasure to _____ and _____ some of you for several years now. Others, I have only _____ a few times, and some of you not at all. No matter, I still think you are all a bunch of _____. It wouldn't surprise me if one day management realized what an _____ each one of you is and decided to _____ you!

(Deliver an emotional finish).

I will _____ forget my long years at _____. And all of you will be _____ to forget. I hope each and every one of you gets the _____ you deserve! I know you all think I've been a _____ in the _____. You all know that I'm pretty _____ up most of the time. Some of you probably think I should just _____ up and _____ away. But I'm sure most of you think I should just go to _____. You probably think I should take this new job and stick it _____ my _____. And I will!

In closing, I would like to leave you with the words of a great philosopher:

"Life is like the core of the apple; it never gets into the pie."

(Pause for applause, smile briefly, sit down, avoid paying for your meal).

I cleared my throat loudly to get everybody's attention. "Okay," I said, "let me see if I can do this."

And here is the master copy of the speech that I read aloud with the blanks filled in:

ACME Speech Company

Speech Number 235: Farewell Luncheon

(Act surprised, stand up, clear throat, begin talking in a clear voice).

Well, this is a surprise! I have been with **SCSU Corp** for **five** very **good** years. In that time, I have **met** and **worked with** a lot of **nice** people. Some of the people were real **serious;** others were very **fun** to work with and made me **laugh.** But, on the whole, I think most people at **SCSU Corp** are pretty **intelligent** and full of **energy.** Overall, I never worked with a group of **people** who were more **professional.**

(Remember to speak clearly and use expansive gestures).

I will be very **sorry** to leave **SCSU Corp**. And I know all of you will be **sorry** to see me leave. It will be **hard** for the company to fill my position because it is **hard** to find somebody who knows his **job** from a **professional perspective** in the **first place**. When they do find some **person** to take my place, please treat that person with the same amount of **respect** that you treated me. Remember, that person will have a very **tough** job and will need all of the **help** s/he can get. Overall, treat the new **person** as you would have treated me, but don't end up **puffing up** his **ego**.

(If you are still nervous, imagine your audience is in their underwear).

It's been my pleasure to **know** and **work with** some of you for several years now. Others, I have only **worked with** a few times, and some of you not at all. No matter, I still think you are all a bunch of **great people**. It wouldn't surprise me if one day management realized what an **asset** each one of you is and decided to **promote** you!

(Deliver an emotional finish).

I will **never** forget my long years at **SCSU Corp.** And all of you will be **hard** to forget. I hope each and every one of you gets the **promotion** you deserve! I know you all think I've been a **great friend** in the **past**. You all know that I'm pretty **psyched** up most of the time. Some of you probably think I should just **wise** up and **not go** away. But I'm sure most of you think I should just go to **my new job**. You probably think I should take this new job and stick it **out** my **friends**. And, I will!

In closing, I would like to leave you with the words of a great philosopher:

"Life is like the core of the apple; it never gets into the pie."

(Pause for applause, smile briefly, sit down, avoid paying for your meal).

From the very start, the speech was a big hit. People laughed uproariously at each of the gags. I paused slightly when I got to each of the blanks and then said the words that turned the seemingly nasty phrases into innocent ones. I was rewarded with thunderous outbursts of spontaneous laughter again and again. When I finished, the room erupted into wild applause. *Better to burn out than to fade away. Yeah, that's for sure!*

Logan looked stricken several times while I was reading the speech. When I finished, I noticed that his face was very red. He suddenly pulled out his cell phone, looked at it, and said to anybody who was within earshot: "Sorry, I've got to take this." Logan left the conference room and did not come back. His absence was hardly noticed as the party continued.

Much later, I was packing up the last of the items on my desk when Peggy dropped in to say goodbye.

"Really gonna miss you, bud!" she said with a smile. "Guess you are not gonna miss Logan."

"Nope," I said putting my The Far Side desk calendar into the box of belongings.

"I overheard Logan talking to Mr. Trowel. He thinks your speech was a direct criticism of him and his management style."

"What? How could he possibly have thought that?" I asked as I unpinned my favorite Dilbert cartoons from my cubicle wall and dropped them into the box. "That speech was absolute nonsense."

"I don't know, but his face got redder and redder as each of your gags got a laugh," Peggy said with a smile. "I guess he thought that they were all aimed at him."

Wow, I thought, *you really never know what lens somebody is going to use to filter information*. I was just trying to be funny, but Logan had been reading between the lines. He thought that I was saying *Take this job and shove it*. But all I was really saying was *Don't worry, be happy!*

This Page Intentionally Left Blank[1]

---

[1] Except, of course, for the notice in the center of the page. And except for this footnote. The line above the footnote is also an exception. The page number is too. Other than the aforementioned, this page is definitely blank.

SOC4 SHAKE THAT THING

Warning: Before you commit to reading this entire piece, you should be aware that you will be required to perform a specific task when you reach the end of it. Your participation will not be optional; you will be *required* to act. But don't worry. What you will have to do will be so entertaining, and you will be so curious about the results, that you will not mind doing it at all. You have been warned!

Early one fine morning, I was sitting at my desk in my comfortable office sifting through emails on my desktop PC. To the right of my keyboard, I had a steaming mug of hot coffee and a paper plate with a toasted bagel smeared with low-fat cream cheese. Halfway through my email review, a large, overly toasted crumb fell from the bagel that I was hefting towards my mouth and landed on the keyboard in the slot between the I, O, L, and K keys. I put the bagel down and gingerly tried to retrieve the crumb. But I fat-fingered the crumb such that it split in half and both pieces fell through the crack and into the keyboard.

I got a pencil from my desk drawer and tried to pry the crumbs out. But instead of coming out, they split into several smaller pieces that just sat there beneath the I, O, L, and K keys. Now I was thoroughly annoyed. Those crumbs had to come out—and come out now! There was no way that I could continue to work on vetting emails with those bagel crumbs sitting inside my keyboard, taunting me.

So, I moved the coffee mug and the paper plate aside and picked up the keyboard. I turned it upside down and shook it. Then, keeping it upside down and at a 45-degree angle, I first banged the left side on my desk and then banged the right side on my desk. I did this several times. Then I shook the inverted keyboard violently a few more times.

The results of my actions were as astounding as they were disgusting! Not only did I dislodge the bagel bits, but a plethora of bizarre debris covered the top of the desk in front of my monitor. There were bagel crumbs from today and from breakfasts past, hairs, bits of dust, unidentifiable small white things (*dandruff or maybe dried skin?*), orange pencil eraser crumbs, a dead bug, a fingernail clipping, a few sesame seeds, two staples (one closed and one open), and assorted dried crumbs from countless lunches I had eaten at my desk. I had no idea that so much stuff had made its way beneath the keys over the years. It took me a few minutes to sweep every vestige of that amazing debris field off of my desk and into my trash can.

Okay, so now it is time for the *reader participation* part of this piece. Put this book down and go to your desktop PC. Pick up the keyboard and flip it upside down. Shake that thing. Shake it violently. Then, keeping it at a 45-degree angle, bang the left side against the surface of the desk several times. Do the same thing with the right side. Then, keeping the keyboard inverted, shake it several more times over your desktop. Put the keyboard aside and take a moment to survey the flotsam and jetsam that litters your desk before you sweep it into a trashcan. Pretty disgusting, right? Right!

ABOUT THE AUTHOR

Michael A. Raithel works as a senior systems analyst for the premier contract research organization in the Washington, DC area. He has been a computer programmer in mainframe, UNIX, Linux, and Windows environments in both the commercial and government sectors since 1980. Michael has written five books on SAS software usage and is the author of more than 25 SAS technical papers. He is a popular lecturer at SAS Global Forum, regional SAS conferences, and at local SAS users groups. A copy of his first book, *Tuning SAS Applications in the MVS Environment*, resides in the Smithsonian Institution of American History's Permanent Research Collection of Information Technology.

Michael is a lifelong gym rat and avid runner. He has completed 10 marathons including the 2013 and 2014 Boston Marathons, the 2014 Tokyo Marathon, and the 2015 London Marathon. He would have written a longer bio, but he had to run.

You can follow Michael on *LinkedIn*, access all of his SAS publications via **http://tinyurl.com/jkufjxx** , or drop him a nice note at maraithel@gmail.com

This is the last page of the book. That is obvious in the e-book edition. But it is not so obvious in the print edition because the Amazon CreatSpace book printing process automatically adds a couple of *control* pages beyond what I have written.

If I had been more verbose then the book would have ended with *About the Author* being the *folium versum* and this page would not even exist. The same thing would have happened if I had been more concise. The font size played a role too. If I had used 10-point Palatino Linotype, then the book would have been shorter. With 12-point, it would have been longer. But no; I decided to use 11-point Palatino Linotype for the best readability. Consequently, this page's very existence is pure happenstance.

Many authors leave the last page of their books blank, which essentially cheats their readers out of a page that they have paid for. But, that is just not me. There is no way that I would ever consider inflating the value of my book by giving my readers one page less than what they bought.

Instead, I am going to provide a last page that both you and I can be proud of. It will be a last page with lots of words on it. Those words will express ideas and connect them in interesting and novel ways. My goal is for you to smile and say to yourself: "That is the best non-blank last page of a book I have ever read!"

Giving you your money's worth does present me with an issue, though. All of my remaining computer programmer-related stories are longer--much longer--than a single page. If I were to start relating one of them here, then I would either have to cut it off at the end of this page, or add additional pages. The former would be unsatisfying to you, while the latter would mean that this would no longer be the last page of the book.

44510743R00095